Praise for *Future on Fire*

"At last, a book that can be shared with anyone awakening to the urgency of climate justice. In clear and accessible prose, *Future on Fire* shows us why we are in an ecological crisis—and what it will take to move beyond it. With meticulous care, David Camfield lays out sharp and compelling arguments for building mass movements that set their sights on ecosocialism. Spread the word!"
—David McNally, Cullen Distinguished Professor of History and Business, University of Houston, and author of *Global Slump* and *Monsters of the Market*

"Naomi Klein says only mass movements can save us from climate catastrophe. In this clear, concise, and absolutely convincing book, David Camfield shows why that is, and how we can build an effective movement to stop capitalism's deadly assault on our planet. Essential reading for every climate activist."
—Ian Angus, author of *Facing the Anthropocene* and editor of climateandcapitalism.com

"In these times of rising oceans and constant bruising of the natural world it is easy to feel hopeless and alone. David Camfield's fine-grained study shows precisely where the resources for hope lie: in collective mass movements that threaten capitalism's power and its planet-destroying drive for profit. It is essential reading for all those seeking to put the brakes on accumulation, but especially for those who dare to imagine a world of beauty and justice."
—Tithi Bhattacharya, coauthor of *Feminism for the 99%*

"Facing up to the climate crisis means building mass movements, but what does this entail? David Camfield has given activists an indispensable guide to the key issues and the practical implications."
—Gareth Dale, coeditor of *Green Growth: Ideology, Political Economy and the Alternatives*

"This book is a powerfully concise and brilliant primer on the connections between climate change and capitalism, and the potential of social movements. Camfield weaves in lessons from history, dispels false solutions to the crisis, and lays out clear opportunities. Perfect for climate justice organizers and climate strikers thinking through strategy and what it will take to win the world we so urgently need."
—James Hutt, labour and climate organizer, digital campaign strategist

"We know what the solutions are—David Camfield asks the question we should all be focusing on now: what is stopping policymakers from acting? Camfield argues that we—the workers, students, and caregivers of civil society—have a critical role to play—not as consumers or even primarily as voters, but as builders of mass movements. It is a compelling argument for the power we hold when we organize collectively. This book is illuminating, empowering, and hopeful."
—Hannah Muhajarine, organizer with Manitoba Energy Justice Coalition

Future on Fire
Capitalism and the Politics of Climate Change

David Camfield

FP

Fernwood Publishing

Halifax and Winnipeg

Future on Fire: Capitalism and the Politics of Climate Change
David Camfield
This edition © 2023 PM Press.

ISBN: 978–1–62963–937–6
Library of Congress Control Number: 2021945064

Cover design by Drohan DiSanto
Interior design by briandesign

10 9 8 7 6 5 4 3 2 1

PM Press
PO Box 23912
Oakland, CA 94623
www.pmpress.org

Published in Canada by Fernwood Publishing
32 Oceanvista Lane, Black Point, Nova Scotia, B0J 1B0
and 748 Broadway Avenue, Winnipeg, Manitoba, R3G 0X3
www.fernwoodpublishing.ca

Fernwood Publishing Company Limited gratefully acknowledges the financial support of the Government of Canada, the Canada Council for the Arts, the Manitoba Department of Culture, Heritage and Tourism under the Manitoba Publishers Marketing Assistance Program and the Province of Manitoba, through the Book Publishing Tax Credit, for our publishing program. We are pleased to work in partnership with the Province of Nova Scotia to develop and promote our creative industries for the benefit of all Nova Scotians.

Library and Archives Canada Cataloguing in Publication

Title: Future on fire : capitalism and the politics of climate change /
David Camfield.
Names: Camfield, David, author.
Description: Includes index.
Identifiers: Canadiana (print) 2021034041X | Canadiana (ebook) 20210363061 |
ISBN 9781773635132 (softcover) | ISBN 9781773635323 (EPUB) |
ISBN 9781773635330 (PDF)
Subjects: LCSH: Ecosocialism.
Classification: LCC HX550.E25 C36 2021 | DDC 304.2—dc23

"Only mass social movements can save us now."
—Naomi Klein

Contents

Acknowledgments

Although I had been thinking and teaching about the issues explored in this book before the mobilization for the September 2019 global climate strike, it was that experience which pushed me to take on this project. In addition to the encouragement provided by that global mobilization, I have been inspired in the city where I live by people in Manitoba Youth for Climate Action, Manitoba Adults for Climate Action, and subsequently the Manitoba Energy Justice Coalition. Thanks to Gareth Dale, Sunny Enkin Lewis, Hannah Muhajarine, and David Gray-Donald for comments on a draft, to James Hutt for thoughts arising from reading a draft, to Stefan Kipfer and Félix Boggio Éwanjé-Épée for corresponding with me about the *gilets jaunes* movement, and to James Wilt and Simon Pirani for help with sources. Thanks to everyone at PM Press for welcoming this book and seeing it through to publication. Without the skilled physiotherapy of Lesa Campbell I could not have written this book.

Foreword

Dharna Noor

In summer 2021, amid a record-breaking heat wave, a wildfire burned down the entire village of Lytton, British Columbia. In just fifteen minutes' time, the first few wisps of smoke turned to a ravaging inferno.[1] Harrowing footage showed residents jumping into their cars in an attempt to escape, but some found that the town was so surrounded by flames that there was nowhere to go. One man watched in panic as his family home went up in flames, killing his parents. "There was nothing we could do. It came in so fast, we had nowhere to go," he told a local news station.[2]

The implications of climate inaction aren't waiting for us in some far-off future; they're here right now. Extreme temperatures, fires, floods, storms, and droughts are becoming commonplace and all the more deadly. The world is losing some 150 species to extinction every single day, many of them to climate change.[3] Famine, war, and poverty are becoming increasingly common, and the climate crisis is fueling all of them. If emissions continue apace, things will get far, far worse. But as David Camfield explains in this urgent book, if we harness the power of mass movements, that doesn't have to be our fate.

The stakes couldn't be higher, especially for poor and working-class people who face the gravest danger. Due to webs of economic oppression, the largest polluters on the planet tend to suffer less, while those who contribute the least—low-income populations, working-class people, the

Global South—are tragically the most affected. Yet no one is safe, for no region will be untouched by climate change.[4] Typhoons, after all, can topple even the tallest penthouses. Still, somehow, leaders refuse to act.

Is it a lack of scientific research that's responsible for this deadly stubbornness? Are powerful people misguided or confused? In this important book, David Camfield skillfully shows that the issue isn't a lack of information or understanding. Rather, it's our cancerous economic system of extractive, fossil-fueled capitalism that values the short-term growth of profits above all else.

People are demanding decisive climate policy. Public concern about the climate crisis is growing, and scientists' call for action has reached a fever pitch. Due to their decades of pushing the world toward catastrophe, energy giants face not only protests and lawsuits from environmentalists but also campaigns from their own shareholders who say reducing emissions will keep their investments safe. Even the International Energy Agency—an organization founded by Henry Kissinger—says the world must immediately ramp down fossil fuel production.

In this atmosphere, corporate executives have started to talk like climate activists. Google says it's working to "confront climate change head-on."[5] Facebook professes its desire for a "just and equitable transition to a zero-carbon economy."[6] Amazon claims it's "committed to building a sustainable business for our customers and the planet."[7] Even the companies most responsible for causing the climate crisis say they'll play a central role in solving it. ExxonMobil, Shell, BP, and Chevron—the most carbon-polluting corporations of all time— have all announced plans to achieve carbon neutrality. So have meat purveyors, car manufacturers, airlines, for-profit utilities, and other major emitters.

At first blush, this new rhetoric seems to indicate a seismic shift, a sign that amid public pressure, the global elite have all come to their senses. But beneath the shiny veneer of climate pledges are the same old destructive business plans. Energy companies' proposals, which are full of accounting tricks and faith in unproven technologies, don't come close to meeting even the most conservative goals set by international climate policy.[8] Tech firms wax poetic about climate justice while continually signing contracts with top polluting sectors to mutually boost their profits. Planet-warming emissions are still on the rise.[9]

Corporations aren't the only ones responsible for these useless charades. Government actors have also failed to take these companies to account. Despite decades of evidence that companies are blatantly unwilling to compromise their business models for the sake of planetary survival, state actors have largely avoided imposing even moderate regulations. Moreover, they continually reward ruinous corporate behavior with multibillion-dollar tax breaks and subsidies.[10]

Some things have changed. Due to the shifting tides of the energy market and the demands of climate activists, politicians are putting forth more comprehensive environmental policies than ever before. Some frameworks, like the Green New Deal, could be transformative if passed. But so far, enacted plans amount to tinkering hopelessly around the edges of the radical changes we need.

Without profound cuts to greenhouse gas emissions, the death toll from heat waves alone may eclipse that of all infectious diseases combined.[11] The world's ice sheets will continue to melt and pour into the oceans, swallowing coastal communities.[12] Insect plagues will spawn food shortages.[13] All the while, the already-chasmic global wealth gap will grow wider, leaving those without means little chance of survival.[14]

Scientifically speaking, we know what we must do: We must phase out of coal, oil, and gas at once, reshape our transit systems and housing plans, design a more humane and sustainable food system, decarbonize every sector of the economy. Politically, though, this can seem like an impossible undertaking.

Future on Fire is essential reading for those looking for a way to make these shifts and build a more just world. Camfield illuminates the uncharted territory before us with lessons gleaned from past political projects. He also gives readers a north star: achieving ecosocialism.

1.

The Path We're On

Since you're reading this book, you won't need to be convinced that Earth's climate is changing rapidly because of human activity. It's widely known that greenhouse gas (GHG) emissions have caused the global average surface temperature to rise by over 1°C above the preindustrial levels measured during the second half of the 1800s.[1] What's less well understood is that current government policies for reducing emissions still set Earth on a path toward between 2.5 and 2.9° warming above preindustrial levels by 2100. That kind of heating is far above the maximum of 2° and the preferred limit of 1.5° agreed to in the United Nations (UN) Paris Accord of 2015.[2] Worse, that estimate of disastrous warming by the end of the century assumes that future GHG pollution levels will actually reflect today's government policies for lowering emissions, in spite of the record of emissions often exceeding targets.

To put those numbers in perspective, we should heed ecological researcher Andreas Malm: "Consider the 2 degrees target, not as a threshold to dangerous global warming—we are well within its field of force—but rather as a demarcation between the dangerous and the extremely dangerous, beyond which positive feedback mechanisms might run amok. To have at least a reasonable chance of maintaining an orderly civilization, we should the keep the rise in average temperature below that line."[3]

We can't be certain that 2° is the line between dangerous and extremely dangerous warming; that figure comes from the UN's Intergovernmental Panel on Climate Change (IPCC), whose "gold-standard" scientific reports are "conservative, integrating only new research that passes the threshold of inarguability."[4] Some scientists argue that the climate science models on which the IPCC relies may underestimate what will happen if emissions continue to grow a lot in the coming decades, and that they may also be inaccurate beyond 2100. There is a risk that even 2° of warming could set off feedback processes—such as the large-scale thawing of permafrost, which stores enormous quantities of GHGs, or the loss of ice sheets in Greenland or the Arctic—that would lead to global temperatures rising faster than those models predict. Such feedbacks would lock Earth into runaway warming, with temperatures continuing to rise no matter how much emissions from human activity were slashed.[5] As writer Richard Seymour points out, "The problem with ecological feedbacks and tipping points is that, while their existence is well established thanks to the work of paleoclimatologists, it would be impossible to say when and how they would appear. You wouldn't know it was coming until it had happened already."[6] It's probably still possible to avoid extremely dangerous levels of climate change and runaway warming, but it will take drastic cuts in GHG emissions that start soon.

Heating is already having negative effects on the Earth System (a term that reflects many scientists' understanding of how different natural processes are part of a complex integrated whole). The more the planet warms, the worse these will get. People are beginning to experience these effects all over the world. It's not just that average temperatures are rising; extreme weather is also becoming more common. Extreme events like heat waves, high winds, and downpours of rain are happening more often. As the atmosphere changes, severe cold spells are becoming more common in some places. Periods of hot, dry weather are becoming longer and more common. These, in turn, are fueling more and larger wildfires.

Some land is becoming drier, while dry land is becoming desert. Sea levels are rising and will continue to rise. Flooding will grow, along with more landslides. Glaciers will melt, leading to river flows shrinking and changing the timing of those flows. We have only just begun to see how all this is altering ecosystems globally.

Sadly, climate change is not the end of the story of how human society is changing the Earth System. Many processes are being affected. What some scientists call "change in biosphere integrity"—the extinction of many animal and plant species—is being driven by climate change and other consequences of human activity. This mass extinction is a serious problem for humans because of how we depend on the rest of nature for life. Some people's ways of life are being undermined by the disappearance of animal populations, whether in water or on land. We are all threatened by the decline of insect populations that pesticides and the destruction of habitats have caused; without pollinators, agriculture would collapse. In addition, oceans are becoming more acidic; flows of phosphorous and nitrogen from industrial agriculture into water and soils are swelling; forest cover is shrinking; freshwater is being depleted; there are higher levels of aerosols (fine particles) in the air; and many harmful or potentially harmful chemicals and other substances are being spewed into the environment. In sum, "The relatively stable, 11,700-year-long Holocene epoch, the only state of the planet that we know for certain can support contemporary human societies, is now being destabilized."[7] Some scientists conclude we are now living in a new epoch in the long history of the Earth System, the Anthropocene.[8] Others prefer to describe what is happening as a global ecological crisis.

Deadly Consequences

Whatever we call it, what we are doing to the rest of nature is having deadly consequences for humans that will definitely get much worse. In the memorable words of researcher Eddie Yuen, "The question is no longer whether there will be environmental catastrophes, but for whom."[9] A vast and growing torrent of studies attempts to predict what climate change and, to a lesser extent, other human-driven changes to the Earth System will mean for people. For example, one team of researchers reports:

> We found traceable evidence for 467 pathways by which human health, water, food, economy, infrastructure and security have been recently impacted by climate hazards such as warming, heatwaves, precipitation, drought, floods, fires, storms, sea-level rise and changes in natural land cover and ocean chemistry. . . . Ongoing climate change will pose a heightened threat to humanity that will be greatly aggravated if substantial and timely reductions of GHG emissions are not achieved.[10]

Hotter temperatures alone will kill many people. The heat waves that took the lives of fifty-five thousand people in Russia in 2010 and thirty-five thousand across Europe in 2003 give us some sense of what this will look like.[11] More frequent extremely hot weather will also kill through the spread of disease and by making it harder for people to get enough food and clean water. People in several regions of the Global South will be most severely affected by global warming. The threat is, however, not limited to those regions. Internationally, it is poor people and elderly people who are most vulnerable. The direct effects of heat alone are not the only threat. Other kinds of extreme weather can also be lethal. Rising waters will displace many people. In some cases, ocean levels swelled by the changing climate will be the immediate culprit. This is the case for many coastal areas. The Miami metropolitan area of Florida, where some six million people live, is one region in a rich country where rising seas will displace people. As the author Ashley Dawson has pointed out, "Given the highly vulnerable infrastructure that weaves through cities, once one part of the metropolis has to be abandoned because of the rising tides, the city will for all practical purposes cease to function. How, for example, would elevated portions of Miami continue to function without access to clean water or sewage?"[12] Yet the problems facing Miami are dwarfed by those facing many coastal cities in the Global South. For example, Jakarta, with ten million people in a larger urban region in Indonesia of over thirty million, is sinking because of how groundwater is being used at an unsustainable rate. There are thirteen rivers in the city but they are terribly polluted. At the same time the city faces rising sea levels.[13]

Why Social Arrangements Matter

The example of how heat waves kill helps us to understand why it's wrong to think of "climate change" affecting "people" in a simple and straightforward way. There is no doubt that it has far-reaching effects, but it always affects people in the context of the specific society in which they live. How a society is organized is fundamental to how climate change affects people. Poverty makes this obvious: if during a heat wave you can't get enough drinkable water and access to a cool space because you can't afford to pay for them, your chances of survival are generally much lower. Similarly, people who are compelled to work for pay in dangerously hot conditions, because they need the money to survive and they won't get paid if they don't work, are suffering because of how their society is organized.

The same is true when it comes to climate change and migration. As rising waters, drought, and other effects of climate change drive more people to move, the impact on people will vary depending on their wealth and power. Who can get to safety before the storm hits the city and who must remain behind; who can move from the countryside into the city and find decent housing and who can only build a shack; who can get a visa to cross a border legally and who must risk entry without papers; who can buy a plane ticket and who can only board an overcrowded ship—such things are decided by how societies are organized, not by the climate.

As the climate changes, social arrangements will determine how many people will die and who they will be. They will also determine what adaptation to climate change will look like and who will pay for it. The impact on people will reflect the degree to which the sanctity of profit-making and the power of corporate owners reign supreme in a society. How racism, sexism, and other forms of oppression shape societies will also influence how climate change affects people.

We can clearly see how the organization of society makes all the difference by comparing how Haiti and Cuba have been affected by storms. The two countries are in the same region of the Caribbean. In the three decades after 1980 Haiti was hit by twenty-three hurricanes and thirty-five floods. In Cuba there were twenty-seven hurricanes and twenty floods over those years. Cuba and Haiti have similar population sizes, but the death toll in Haiti—between 6,666 and 8,608 people—was vastly larger than the 193–203 killed in Cuba. Why the stark difference? Haiti has long suffered at the hands of imperialism, from the debt burden and diplomatic isolation imposed by France and the US in the early 1800s as punishment for the overthrow of slavery to the neoliberal policies of the International Monetary Fund and World Bank.[14] As a result, dire poverty is rampant and public services are extremely weak. In contrast, Cuba's civil defense, early warning and public health systems, along with its level of infrastructure development—all consequences of the Cuban Revolution of 1959—provide its citizens with much greater protection from extreme weather.[15]

The basic point that social arrangements shape how climate change affects people is usually either missed entirely

or barely considered by research studies that attempt to predict
its impacts. Yet it is absolutely crucial. Such research generally
constructs simple models. For example, "rapid climate change
→ resource conflict → social breakdown → violence." But, as
researchers Joel Wainwright and Geoff Mann argue:

> notwithstanding an impressive body of literature that
> draws correlations between discrete effects of climate
> change (such as more or less rain) and social conflict
> (more or less fighting), social scientists are a long way
> from being able to establish the "truth" of any of these
> simple causal models. Certainly these models cannot
> be scaled up from empirical cases to support meaning-
> ful claims about the future of the entire planet. There
> are simply too many analytical problems involved.[16]

As Ashley Dawson suggests, "efforts to conjure up future
worlds based on unknowable contingencies and discon-
tinuous ramifications" are unreliable. Visions of climate
apocalypse often reflect the "present-day investments and
bugaboos" of our rulers and those who see the world through
their eyes.[17]

However, as Wainwright and Mann contend, "The impos-
sibility of accurate prediction does not mean we should
throw up our hands and give up trying to anticipate a range
of futures. Instead, the challenge of all climate futures centers
on the question of the political. How the world will respond
politically to climate change and its effects"[18] is the critical
question. To be clear, the issue here is not just what governments and other state institutions do, although what states
do is extremely important. The essence of politics is power in
society. Political responses to climate change are about how
groups of people wield power to organize society.

This means we are not all in it together. Malm explains:
"Witness [Hurricane] Katrina in black and in white neighborhoods of New Orleans, [Hurricane] Sandy in Haiti

and in Manhattan, sea level rise in Bangladesh and in the Netherlands. . . . For the foreseeable future—indeed, as long as there are class [meaning class-divided] societies on earth— there *will* be lifeboats for the rich and privileged, and there will *not* be any shared sense of catastrophe."[19]

There is no better clue of what this may look like than Eko Atlantic. This is a city being built on a newly constructed island just off the coast of Africa's biggest city, Lagos. Its developers bill it as "reversing coastal erosion," protected from the rising Atlantic ocean by "a sea wall built to last 1,000 years" that will allow it to be "a solution to the chronic shortage of prime real estate in Lagos, and the need for a new financial headquarters for Nigeria—the largest economy in Africa."[20] When finished, it is expected to have 250,000 residents. But what will this new city mean for the very poor people, struggling to get by in the informal economy, who make up most of the multimillion residents of Lagos? They will not be living in Eko Atlantic's well-serviced apartment towers. Journalist Martin Lukacs suggests that "Eko Atlantic is where you can begin to see a possible future—a vision of privatized green enclaves for the ultra rich ringed by slums lacking water or electricity, in which a surplus population scramble for depleting resources and shelter to fend off the coming floods and storms."[21]

Why Are We on This Path?

We can't avoid asking the question "why are we on this path?" In spite of everything that has been known for decades about climate change and its consequences, why have governments failed to take decisive action to reduce emissions? Why are we headed toward close to 3° of warming by the end of this century along with a broader ecological crisis? As historian Simon Pirani suggests, "In a century's time, when the impacts of global warming will be much more ruinous than they are today, people may look back at this failure as collective madness. There may be an analogy with the way people today view Europe's descent in to the barbaric slaughter of the First World War, a century ago, as collective madness. It *was* madness, but it had definite political, social and economic causes."[22] The same is true for the path we're on to extremely dangerous climate change and a worsening ecological crisis.

One common explanation is that global population growth is responsible for the ongoing rise in GHG emissions and for other kinds of environmental destruction.[23] However, there is no direct connection between the number of people on the planet and the emissions that are changing Earth's climate or other ways in which the Earth System is being disrupted. Individuals don't spew GHGs into the environment or consume resources except as part of the society to which they belong. As Pirani notes, "fossil fuels are consumed by and through technological systems, which are in turn situated in social and economic systems."[24] Rich, advanced countries of the North burn much more fossil fuel than the much larger and faster-growing populations of the South. When it comes to the pollution of the atmosphere by carbon dioxide (CO_2), methane, and other GHGs, it's not the absolute number of people that's causing the problem. What counts above all else is how societies burn fossil fuels to generate energy.[25] To a lesser extent, other drivers of GHG pollution also matter: the scale of industrial agriculture and the destruction of forests. Population growth is also not the cause of other dimensions of the ecological crisis.

Another common explanation is economic growth. But simply looking at gross domestic product (GDP) statistics and emissions levels or other ecological effects ignores the question of what's going on behind the GDP numbers. It "exclude[s] analysis of energy flows through technological systems."[26] It fails to ask what it is about how society is organized to produce goods and services that leads to GHG emissions, mass extinction, ocean acidification and other problems. Researcher

Gareth Dale points out that "growth is not its own cause." He adds, "The relentless increase in global resource throughput and environmental despoliation is not principally the result of states aspiring to a metric—higher GDP—but of industrial and financial firms, driven by market competition to expand turnover, develop new products, and increase profits."[27]

This points us to the answer to why we're headed toward extremely dangerous warming as part of a deepening ecological crisis. We live in a world in which most goods and services, from food to electricity to entertainment, are produced as commodities; they must be bought. Most commodities are produced by privately owned firms (some are state-owned). The goal of production is profit, not providing people with useful things. The goods and services produced are just a means to that end. Whether large or small, companies are caught up in competition with each other; a company that doesn't bring in enough money can be swallowed up by another firm or driven out of business altogether. Competition compels firms to increase productivity or go under. To make and distribute products, firms hire people, who are forced to sell their ability to work to employers for lack of viable alternative ways of supporting themselves and their dependents. People are able to work for capitalists (the people who control firms and employ most of the rest of us) in large part because of the unpaid labor that's done at home, mostly by women, to raise children and keep today's wageworkers functioning. These are capitalism's defining characteristics.

Capitalism is not a mental paradigm. Nor is it just an economic system. It's a way of organizing society, an "institutionalized social order."[28] Its historical emergence and spread involved violently depriving people of access to the land or water on which they had been able to rely for subsistence and also undermining the independence of artisans. These processes of dispossession continue today. They have created an enormous global working class. This encompasses everyone who sells their ability to work in exchange for pay and has little or no management authority, regardless of whether they are employed full-time or part-time, regularly or irregularly, for high pay or low. It also includes unwaged people who rely on the wages of others. The mental and manual labor of this working class produces the commodities that are the source of business profits; because the value of what workers produce is vastly greater than the wages and benefits they're paid, the working class as a whole is exploited by capital.[29]

Although wood, water, and peat were important sources of energy in the earliest phase of capitalism in Europe, capitalism was powered by fossil fuels as it developed and spread around the world in the 1800s. Coal-fueled steam power came first. Capitalists in Britain, where capitalism first emerged, opted for steam, "laying the foundation of the fossil economy," "because it augmented the power of some over others," as Malm's pathbreaking research has uncovered. "The succession of fossil-fuelled technologies following steam—electricity, the internal combustion engine, the petroleum complex: cars, tankers, refineries, petrochemicals, aviation . . . —have all been introduced through investment decisions, sometimes with crucial input from certain governments but rarely through democratic deliberation."[30] Fossil fuels became "embedded in every aspect" of capitalism, putting society on the path to disastrous climate change.[31]

Capitalism is also the underlying cause of the other dimensions of the global ecological crisis. Capitalist competition drives the scale of commodity production to expand without limits. Yet nature is not infinite. The cancer-like growth of profit-driven production is disrupting ecosystems, killing species, and depleting finite resources. The pace of capitalist production is also ever-increasing. The faster capital can move through cycles of investment, production, sale, profit, and reinvestment, the more money firms can make. The speed of capital accumulation races far beyond the speeds at which nature replenishes—think of forests cut down faster than new trees can be grown, or soil depleted of nutrients because it isn't left fallow.[32]

Capitalism is ultimately responsible for the obstacles that are keeping us on the path to extremely dangerous climate change. Most oil, natural gas, and coal are extracted by profit-driven companies. Most electricity is generated by for-profit firms too. The companies that build vehicles and make machinery and everything else that is part of society's energy system are in it for profit. Three environmental studies researchers state the truth when they write that "the existing investments made by fossil fuel interests are simply too great, their profits too astronomical . . . and the diversity of their product too limited for them to undermine their own ability to hold on to this status quo . . . perhaps never before has there been an industry with so much power and so much to lose through domestic and international policymaking."[33]

Outside the fossil fuel industry itself, many other companies oppose a transition away from fossil energy because it would hurt their profits. This includes banks and other firms with investments in fossil fuels as well as investment funds with a stake in the industry. For example, in Canada there are eight large companies involved in the Alberta tar sands. They are "at the heart of the system of large, monopolistic corporations that shape the Canadian economy . . . [and] Canadian banks . . . are deeply linked to the extraction corporations. . . . The portfolios of most of the large retirement funds or mutual funds in Canada also rely on the value of the securities of extraction companies."[34] The companies with the most to lose from a transition from fossil fuels put a lot of effort into influencing government policy. What's more, the far-reaching public investment in transportation, energy generation, construction, and other spheres that's needed for such a transition is anathema to neoliberal ideology, which still influences governments.[35] Governments also know that making a serious move away from fossil fuels would provoke enormous resistance from at least some major capitalists. Firms could decide to suspend operations or shift investments elsewhere to punish a government that threatened their profits. This could have a ripple effect on other firms and lead financial capital to drive down the value of the country's bonds and currency in international markets. It's capitalism that put us on the road to extremely dangerous warming, and it's capitalism that keeps us from turning in a different direction.

That's Not All Capitalism Has in Store for Us

The focus so far has been on climate change and the ecological crisis. Unfortunately, that's *far* from all that matters about where capitalism is taking us. There are *many* ways in which capitalism, which is inextricably interwoven with many forms of oppression, is harming people today. There are many ways in which it's making people's lives worse. For one, the share of the world's population that eats fewer calories than they need has grown in recent years.[36] There is more than enough food produced, but some people can't afford it. Even in the rich countries, life was getting harder for many people even before the COVID-19 pandemic triggered the worst economic crisis since the Great Depression of the 1930s. A growing share of jobs are worsening as employers make work more intense and less secure. More jobs have nonstandard and often irregular hours. People are taking on more debt and often spending more on making payments even with very low interest rates. Access to services like health care and public transit is often shrinking, and quality is declining. All the while we're bombarded with the message that we must be happy and that unhappiness is pathological. Add in saturation by electronically delivered images and information, factor in spreading awareness of climate change, and is it any wonder that mental distress was spreading even before COVID-19 and the latest economic crisis hit?[37]

These trends aren't new. However, they've been made worse by how, since the Great Recession of 2008–9, capitalism has been mired in what economist Michael Roberts calls "a long depression similar to 1873–97 or 1929–42 . . . an economic environment where investment in productive capital is way below previous average levels, with little sign of pick-up."[38] The COVID-19 pandemic triggered a deep recession, but it was the condition capitalism was in when the pandemic hit that explains why it has been so deep. We can expect the long depression to last until profits from investment revive. That won't happen until economic slumps drive down the cost of labor, get rid of many less-competitive firms, and eliminate a lot of debt—all of which will hurt many people. The long depression has brought with it austerity—"not simply spending cuts" but "a shift in the entire civilisational edifice of capitalism, deepening an equivalent shift that began in the mid-1970s."[39]

"Women have been disproportionately affected by the dismantling and privatisation of public services, in particular the provision of care for children, the disabled, the sick and the elderly, areas in which women perform the majority of the labour, paid and unpaid."[40] In these conditions, racism has been given a boost as some members of dominant racial groups, egged on by some politicians and corporate media outlets, look for scapegoats and seek comfort in nationalist ideas about who "really" belongs. Political forces of the hard right (think of the Republican Party in the US, the Conservative Party in the UK, and the right wing of the Conservatives in Canada) and the far right (fascists and others like Donald Trump who aim to get rid of even the minimal form of democracy that exists in some countries today) have grown stronger. These forces don't only fan the flames of racism; they also target trans people, cis women, and other people who face oppression. In the US and UK, hit hard by the Great Recession and austerity, life expectancy had fallen even before 2020 when the pandemic and the latest recession hit.[41]

It was capitalism that created the ecological and social conditions in which the SARS-CoV-2 virus that causes COVID-19 could become a terrible pandemic. This virus, like most new pathogens (organisms that cause disease), was transmitted from an animal host to humans and then spread rapidly among people. Deforestation, the loss of biodiversity, the expansion of agribusiness—especially capitalist industrial livestock production—and the growth of what were once rural towns into large cities have paved the way for pathogenic organisms like SARS-Co-V-2 to spread from animals to humans. Once that happens, diseases that can spread from human to human are now able to do so as never before because of the forms of interconnectedness built by capitalism: "What were once local spillovers are now epidemics trawling their way through global webs of travel and trade."[42] As long as the ecological and social conditions that promote the transmission of new pathogens from other animals to humans and then between humans persist, we should not expect COVID-19 to be the last global pandemic of a new deadly disease.

This is the path we're speeding along thanks to capitalism. How can we apply an emergency brake and then head in a different direction? At a *minimum*, we need action that slashes GHG emissions *and* does so in ways that address social injustice on a global scale, leaving no one behind. This is what many supporters of climate justice—by which I mean a vision of social change that aims at least to prevent an extremely dangerous level of climate change and at the same time reduce social injustice—call a *just transition*.[43] The IPCC reported in 2018 that to limit warming to 1.5° over preindustrial temperatures global net CO_2 emissions need to drop by some 45 percent below 2010 levels by 2030 and reach net zero around 2050. To have a two-thirds probability of keeping warming below 2° will take a drop of some 25 percent by 2030 and net zero by around 2070. Emissions of other GHGs also need to plunge. This will require "rapid and far-reaching transitions in energy, land, urban and infrastructure (including transport and buildings), and industrial systems" on an "unprecedented" scale.[44]

Fossil fuels will have to be phased out; simply producing more energy from renewable sources will not get us where we need to go. The goal for CO_2 emissions needs to be real zero (no emissions), not net zero (some combination of ongoing CO_2 pollution coupled with schemes for removing it from the atmosphere). As three climate scientists who admit to having been misled by the net zero approach put it, net zero policies "were and still are driven by a need to protect business as usual, not the climate. If we want to keep people safe, then large and sustained cuts to carbon emissions need to happen now."[45] Rich countries will need to reduce their total energy demand at the same time as they slash their GHG emissions. This is because of how quickly fossil fuels have to be phased out, the need for countries in the Global South to use more energy in order to improve people's living standards, and challenges involved in building new nonfossil energy systems. As scientist Stan Cox puts it, in rich countries "it is now necessary to do three things simultaneously: drive emissions down to zero; adapt society to a smaller energy supply while still producing as much nonfossil energy as is required for sustenance and good quality of life; and ensure fair, equitable access to resources and economic security."[46] The technologies needed for such a historic shift already exist; the obstacles lie in how society is organized.[47]

The goal of rapidly slashing emissions in socially just ways is central to some of the various packages of reforms that go under the name of a Green New Deal (GND). In the US, the best-known GNDs are the congressional resolution proposed by Alexandria Ocasio-Cortez and Ed Markey in 2018 and the stronger plan that Bernie Sanders proposed during his bid to become the Democratic Party presidential candidate in 2020. It's important to pay attention to the details of GND plans, since the popularity of these calls for bold action has led some supporters of much less ambitious measures to use GND language. A case in point comes from the Australian state of Victoria. In 2020 the parliament voted in favor of a "GND," but what the Labor Party government delivered will not expand public ownership of energy generation and storage and will probably end up reducing the total public housing stock. This demonstrates why "it's a mistake to think of the GND as a single political project, economic program, or set of policy prescriptions. Rather, there are many competing GNDs, reflecting the array of political and economic actors now participating in debates about climate and ecological crisis."[48] It's with this confusion in mind that the authors of the imaginative and expectations-raising book *A Planet to Win: Why We Need a Green New Deal* call what they are arguing for a "radical GND," in contrast to "faux GND" packages.[49]

To reiterate: drastic and rapid GHG emissions cuts coupled with reforms that reduce injustice—what we can call a radical GND—represent a minimum emergency program. In the rich countries, where most readers of this book live, this needs to include measures to reduce the brutal squeeze global capitalism puts on countries of the South and assist the majority of people in the world to both use more energy and reduce GHG emissions.[50] Winning such a GND in many countries would still not resolve the global ecological crisis. It would not by itself uproot capitalism.[51] Nor would it put an end to the many forms of oppression that are part of the existing social order. In the US, Canada, and other settler-colonial societies these include the oppression of Indigenous peoples, which is rooted in dispossession from "land in all its forms" and involves a "genocidal structure that systemically erases" their "relationships and responsibilities to their ancestral places."[52]

However, winning a genuinely just transition would still be an extraordinary victory that would weaken those sources of harm and open up possibilities for more far-reaching change. Who can get us there?

2.

Will Capitalists Save Us?
What about Governments?

It may be hard to believe, but there are still people who argue that we can count on capitalists to lead us away from disaster. Venture capital firm chair Joel Solomon urges us to believe that "things are not always as they seem. Capitalism need not be the enemy." True, he says, if "piled up into pens managed like factory farms . . . money can start to stink." But "if it is allowed free range to roam and get reconnected to the Earth, it can do amazing and important things."[1] He and like-minded thinkers are confident that socially responsible investors will steer us in the right direction. "Trend lines are clear. Cleaner food, services, transportation, energy, buildings, and money are gaining traction rapidly. . . . Trillions of dollars have begun shifting from the most destructive practices into more generative ones."[2] They believe that rationality and a shift in values will lead businesses away from the drive for unlimited and ever-faster growth. "Patient capital will grow along with the clean money movement. It just makes sense."[3] A harder-edged case for having faith in capitalists emphasizes profits rather than values and virtuous ideas. Climate-friendly investments will be more profitable, and so capital will flow in new directions. "Companies will implement more sustainable processes and procedures or they will lose competitiveness in a world that can no longer tolerate unsustainable behavior," argue environmentalist L. Hunter Lovins and business school academic Boyd Cohen. "Acting to protect the climate will unleash a new energy economy and create the greatest prosperity in history."[4]

We live in a social world in which media industries and many people in positions of influence treat extraordinarily rich founders of massive firms—Steve Jobs, Elon Musk, Jeff Bezos, and Oprah Winfrey, for example—as heroes to be emulated. That explains why faith in salvation by capitalists still has a following. In capitalist culture today, such business owners serve as icons who "hold out the promise that major social problems can be solved in this lifetime with the institutions that already exist. . . . Icons idealize capitalist life, put a spin on it, and reflect back something alluring and grandiose that people nonetheless immediately recognize."[5] Yet there is no more reason to believe that iconic capitalists and their unhyped fellow business owners will lead us on a path away from ecological disaster and social degradation than there is to suppose that positive thinking cures cancer and attracts wealth.[6]

Lovins and Cohen made their confident claim that competition will drive companies away from processes that cause climate change and into a transition to clean energy in a book published in 2011. That year, global CO_2 emissions from fossil fuels and industry totaled 34.4 gigatons. Since then emissions levels have risen, reaching 36.4 gigatons in 2019.[7] Left to their own devices, we can expect capitalists to continue to pollute with CO_2 and other GHGs. To be sure, some will find ways to make considerable profits by investing in renewable energy generation or producing other goods and services that could be useful for addressing the climate crisis. But a rapid, all-embracing transition away from GHG pollution of the kind required to limit climate change to dangerous rather than extremely dangerous levels would not boost the profits of most firms. There is absolutely no way that the drastic and rapid emissions reductions that the IPCC reports say are needed will be achieved by leaving it up to capitalists to mend their ways. Capital won't just stop expanding or slow down the pace of accumulation in order to respect ecological boundaries. Nor will the owners of corporations stop eliminating jobs, reorganizing work in ways that are bad for workers, and searching for ways to make money by charging people for services that were formerly free and public but are now privatized.

As we've seen, people who own or control firms are driven by competition to act in ways that treat ever-higher profits—which companies need in order to invest in new technology and other means of making more money, so that they don't lose market share to rival firms—as the supreme goal even if that means disregarding nature's limits. As David McNally, a leading socialist analyst of capitalism, puts it, the system is "a machine that no one controls. Every agent must conform to its imperatives. Fail to turn an adequate profit and an enterprise will not survive."[8] It's not the values and preferences of individual capitalists (or consumers) that determine how capitalism operates, but the system's competitive, expansionary, ever-faster logic of profit.

A Just Transition from the Parties of the Status Quo?

The evidence that capitalists won't change direction by themselves is overwhelming. That's why most people concerned about climate change and worsening social conditions look to governments to act. Many still hope for effective action from "enlightened" leaders of the "extreme center"[9]: liberal or social democratic political parties that accept not just capitalism but capitalism in its current neoliberal form, in which the proper role of governments is to keep dismantling barriers to corporate profit.[10] The records of top elected officials Barack Obama in the US, Justin Trudeau in Canada, and Francois Hollande in France put this hope to the test.

As president, Obama did cancel a number of leases to drill for oil and gas in the Arctic. He froze new federal leases for coal mining. But as a 2016 report described, "Over the last seven years, President Obama's Administration has offered hundreds of millions of acres of federally managed public lands to corporations for oil, gas, and coal extraction, with tens of millions now under lease.... This fact alone underscores how the Administration has proceeded by and large with business as usual on public lands and waters, weighing the interests of fossil fuel corporations over communities and climate."[11] Obama also presided over an unprecedented expansion of oil and gas extraction by fracking. His record on social injustice was no better. Even in his first two years in office, when his Democrats had commanding majorities in both houses of Congress and there was widespread popular support for a response to the Great Recession that would put the needs of the working-class majority first, Obama's priority was shoring up neoliberal capitalism. Much of his economic stimulus package was made up of tax cuts and credits that did not create jobs. Obama did nothing of any significance to change how the financial sector operated, even allowing executives from the financial services division of the large insurance firm AIG to collect millions of dollars of bonuses after the company had been bailed out with public funds. Obama's health care "reform" left the industry under the control of private insurance companies, which supported the plan, and left many people without access to medical services. Record numbers of migrants were deported from the US during Obama's years in office. Repressive "war on terror" policies rolled out by his predecessor became further entrenched, and the US military continued to wage that "war" abroad.[12] Although we should recognize the "meaning in the election of an African American to the highest office in a nation born and built on the backs of enslaved Black labour, we should not let that acknowledgment cloud our ability to think clearly and tell the truth." For Black people "Obama's presidency . . . represented the painful continuity of racism, discrimination, and inequality that has always been at the center of Black life in America."[13] The appalling experience of Donald Trump's presidency should not obscure Obama's actual record in office. The policies of Joe Biden's administration will not be identical to those of Obama on climate change and many other issues, since it confronts a more difficult domestic and international situation than Obama's did, but there is no reason to think its policies will be better from the perspective of climate justice and social justice more broadly.[14]

Trudeau is a master of the art of appearing to be serious about addressing climate change while implementing policies that promote fossil fuel extraction. The Liberal government's climate plan, which combined "weak emissions targets, promised investment in clean technologies, and a market-based carbon price," was one that oil and gas firms and the rest of corporate Canada could accept, no matter what Trudeau's Conservative opponents said.[15] Further evidence of Trudeau's lack of commitment to a transition from fossil fuels was the federal government's 2018 decision to purchase the Kinder Morgan Trans Mountain pipeline and complete the construction that will allow it to move even more Alberta tar sands oil to the Pacific Ocean for export. Lukacs's simile captures the Trudeau Liberals' approach: "like a nicotine addict insisting that, to build the courage to quit their habit, they had to chainsmoke."[16] The Climate Action Tracker research project rates Canada as "insufficient" when it comes to reducing GHG pollution, "not consistent with holding warming below 2°C."[17] On matters other than GHG emissions the Trudeau government has been similarly intent on continuing down the path of neoliberal capitalist development. It has endorsed using a federal infrastructure bank to subsidize business investment in private-public partnerships to build "toll highways, bridges, high-speed rail, and power transmission projects."[18] Creating opportunities for corporate profit even when the state could build such projects at a lower cost is a classic neoliberal move. The Trudeau government went to great lengths to present itself as a friend of Indigenous peoples, making "reconciliation" into a buzzword. However, this has been cover for pursuing "the unfinished business of colonization,"[19] designed above all to elicit Indigenous consent to more resource extraction on their territories and to a framework of Indigenous rights that would present only minimal obstacles for investors. Trudeau made it clear to many people whose side he is really on when in 2020 he opposed the rail blockades by Indigenous supporters of the Wet'suwet'en opposition to the Coastal GasLink pipeline in British Columbia (BC).[20] His government also forced striking postal workers back to work, continuing the tradition of undermining the already very restricted right to strike of unionized workers in Canada.

What about social democracy? While the Democrats in the US and the Liberals in Canada are parties intimately linked with certain sectors of business, social democratic parties in Europe and similar parties like the New Democratic Party (NDP) in Canada had, and in some cases still have, close ties with unions. Yet they too have embraced or at least accepted the neoliberal status quo (which is why some left-wing critics call them social liberal). France under the presidency of the Socialist Party's Francois Hollande between 2012 and 2017 is typical of what today's social democrats are like in office. The government was officially committed to action on climate change. In practice, though, it promoted highway and airport expansion and failed to push for a shift to renewable energy generation.[21] It implemented a host of repressive "national security" measures that suspended civil liberties, subjecting Muslims to even more targeting by state authorities, stoking everyday racism, and cracking down on environmentalists, workers' rights defenders, and other protesters. Aggressive French military activity continued in the Middle East and Africa. The government's austerity policies included "reducing employer contributions and corporate taxes, entrenching budgetary constraint, supporting the marketization of public services, and encouraging various forms of labour market flexibility."[22]

Lest one think that this experience of conformity is limited to European social democrats, we should remember that although the NDP hasn't formed a federal government in Canada, NDP provincial governments have not deviated from the disastrous path on which capitalism has us. The NDP government of the province of Alberta from 2015 to 2019 actively pushed for pipeline construction to export more tar sands oil, squabbling with the NDP government of BC. For its part, the BC NDP government opposed the Kinder Morgan Trans Mountain pipeline but supported a massive liquefied natural gas project in the province. The BC NDP government's support for the Coastal GasLink pipeline project pitted it against land defenders from the Wet'suwet'en Indigenous nation in the confrontation that led to widely supported solidarity actions that caused economic disruption across Canada in February 2020.[23]

Whether "enlightened" parties of business or social liberals, the record of the parties of the extreme center shows that they will not bring about anything resembling a just transition. Europe's Green Parties have shown themselves to be part of the extreme center too.[24] It's not that the leaders of these parties are ignorant about the science of climate change; they are well informed. They are also aware of the harm that climate change is doing today, and that its effects will become devastating as the planet warms. They are not deaf: they hear the calls to change direction coming from the global movement for climate action. Why, then, do these parties continue to govern in ways that have led us to a much hotter planet? It's because for them a challenge to fossil capital is inconceivable and because they support the capitalist status quo. The actions required to carry through a just transition are incompatible with its rules, to which these parties' leaders are loyal.

Could Green Left Governments Deliver?

Given the failure of governments of the extreme center to launch a just transition, support is growing for bold action by parties and politicians to their left. The GND proposals of US left social democrats Ocasio-Cortez and Sanders have inspired many people with their packages of reforms to slash GHG emissions and improve the lives of ordinary people. These calls for a GND in the US have led to the development of similar GND packages elsewhere. What they have in common is the basic idea of bringing in a large number of reforms that would bring about a just transition. The intent is to do this in ways that improve people's quality of life with a wide range of new public programs, regulations and rights that would tame capitalism. In the US, most supporters of a radical GND hoped that by electing Sanders to the presidency and like-minded Democrats to Congress they could win what they wanted. In the UK, many supporters looked to electing the Labour Party. In Canada, committed proponents often hope that the NDP will change direction, embrace a GND, and go on to form a government, or that the Green Party will do the same. Whatever the country, the basic argument is the same: parties of the extreme center cannot be expected to make the necessary changes, so we need to elect a government that clearly opposes neoliberalism and supports a just transition.

Could this strategy work? To assess it, we need to look at the experience of past left governments pledged to major reforms. Greece's Syriza (Coalition of the Radical Left) is an important recent example. Initially formed as a coalition of various radical left and ecological forces in 2004, it had become a unitary party by the time it won the 2015 general election, which took place after several years of mass working-class struggle against austerity. Although the politics of most of Syriza's leadership had moderated, the party was still pledged to a program that rejected the vicious austerity to which Greece had been subjected and aimed to revive the economy, expand the welfare state, and strengthen democracy. But the government that Syriza formed (along with a minor right-wing but anti-austerity nationalist party whose support it needed for a majority in parliament) quickly betrayed that program and the hopes of the many people in Greece and around the world who looked to this anti-neoliberal left-wing party for a victory against austerity. It took office saddled with a level of public debt that threatened the state's ability to function, a consequence of Greece's subordinate place within the economy of the European Union and the policies of previous Greek and EU governments and international financial institutions. After failing to negotiate debt relief, the government called a referendum on the bailout deal offered by the EU, the European Central Bank, and the IMF, which was a recipe for more austerity. The result was decisive: 61 percent of voters rejected the deal. Instead of using this act of mass defiance to bolster the fight against austerity, the government surrendered: it signed another deal that contained measures even worse than those in the one people had rejected in the referendum. From then until it lost office in 2019, Syriza administered "a giant experiment in neoliberal social engineering and the first demonstration of the authoritarian, disciplinary potential of the eurozone's financial, monetary, and institutional architecture." The outcome was "the defeat of an enormous mobilization that had the potential to begin a sequence of radical social and political change."[25]

Syriza's spectacular failure was not the result of circumstances found only in countries vulnerable to pressure from more powerful neighbors. Devastating austerity measures were not "imposed upon Greece by external force alone"[26]— the Greek capitalist class was also supportive. In any country, a green left government committed to a just transition would confront intense opposition. Some of this would come from fossil fuel companies and capitalists with investments in fossil fuels. As we saw in the first chapter, "perhaps never

before has there been an industry with so much power and
so much to lose through domestic and international policymaking."[27] Owners of other companies whose profits would be
shrunk by measures taken to slash GHG emissions would also
be hostile. Capitalists in general would be upset by policies
that redistributed wealth, put firms under public ownership,
provided guarantees of income support and new jobs to
workers negatively affected by measures that cut emissions,
challenged settler colonialism, or in other ways weakened
their power.

Governments in capitalist societies are always vulnerable
to pressure from corporations. By scaling back investment
or suspending operations altogether, firms can disrupt the
economic activity that employs most wage earners, produces
needed goods and services, and generates tax revenue for
the state. An "investment strike" could cause a societal crisis.
States are also subject to pressure from credit rating agencies.
Their ratings affect the ability of governments to sell bonds,
which is an important way that states raise the money needed
to fund deficit spending. Weak ratings drive up the interest
rate needed to sell bonds and may deter investors from buying
a state's bonds at all. Global markets can also drive down the
value of a country's currency. Thus a green left government
that tried hard to implement reforms could well find itself
forced by the capitalist class to cease and desist.

Capitalists are not the only opponents such a government
would face. Constitutional protection of private property is a
barrier to putting fossil fuel firms under public ownership as
part of an energy system transition. Many states have passed
laws and implemented rules that limit public spending and
in other ways lock in neoliberal policies that are obstacles to
a just transition; some are signatories to international agreements that do the same, including the Maastricht Treaty that
binds the countries whose currency is the euro. Many top civil
servants, judges, and the heads of "national security" agencies,

the military, and the central bank would likely back corporate resistance to just transition reforms. They would try to persuade the government to water down or abandon its efforts, pointing to the risk of unrest and disruption of the capitalist status quo they serve. They could also use their power within state institutions to obstruct the government. In short, the strategy of electing a green left government and counting on it to deliver climate justice rests on a false assumption: that the state is neutral and can be used to implement whatever policy an elected government desires. But states aren't neutral; they're part of the existing social order. In other words, they're capitalist states, no matter who is in government.[28] Governments are in office, not in power. It's not just that capitalists have an immense amount of power in society; unelected high-ranking state officials also do.

To make matters even more difficult for a government committed to a just transition, its progressive measures would also face hostility from politicians and top state bureaucrats in other countries who are opposed to what it stands for. If a green left government's transition moves had direct effects on other countries, the hostility would be all the greater. (The television series *Occupied*, in which a Norwegian government that tries to halt fossil fuel production faces political and military intervention by states reliant on its oil and gas exports, imagines such a scenario.) For all these reasons, getting parties committed to a just transition into office will clearly not be enough.

3.

Mass Movements: Our Only Hope

There are many versions of history that credit a Great Man (occasionally a Great Woman) for momentous change. "Lincoln freed the slaves," "Gandhi won India's independence," and "Franklin Delano Roosevelt gave Americans the New Deal" are just three examples. But this way of explaining major shifts is misleading: it hides the essential role that the actions of millions of everyday people have played in changing society for the better. It's only such popular unrest that could deliver a just transition on the timeline given us by climate science.

Hidden Histories

Take the abolition of slavery in the US. Of course, it's a fact that during the Civil War the Union's president, Abraham Lincoln, championed the Emancipation Proclamation that took effect in 1863. However, Lincoln had not fought consistently against slavery. He was eventually pushed to proclaim a radical measure that expropriated property on a large scale. The "immediate, unplanned, and uncompensated emancipation of four million slaves" "seemed impossible in the 1850s political universe," notes historian David Roediger. Nothing like it had ever happened before. It happened because Lincoln's hand was forced. It was slaves themselves who did the forcing, fleeing "by the thousands, and ultimately, the hundreds of thousands" from their Confederate masters in "uneven, protracted, and thoughtful motion." Many more stayed put

but "resisted plantation labour." This self-activity is what sociologist W.E.B. Du Bois dubbed a "general strike of the slaves."[1]
So while Lincoln obviously put forward the legal document, it
was the actions of slaves themselves, often taking advantage
of opportunities created by Union military forces,[2] that paved
the way for it and made it a political necessity. More broadly,
according to historian Robin Blackburn, the end of slavery
in the Americas "was not just a matter of decrees, laws and
constitutional amendments. . . . Ultimately emancipation, if
it was to be effective, came from below as well as from above,
with slave de-subordination destroying plantation discipline
while legislation denied the slave order the force of law within
a given territory. The de-subordination of the slaves could be
such a powerful factor that only emancipation allowed the
government to get a lever on the situation."[3] Abolition was
not the gift of Great Men.

In recent years there has been a lot of talk about the New
Deal reforms in the US in the 1930s. Bernie Sanders spoke
of "tak[ing] up the unfinished business of the New Deal and
carry[ing] it to completion."[4] The New Deal is also echoed
in the high-profile GND proposals championed by Sanders,
Ocasio-Cortez, and others in the US. Credit for the original
New Deal is usually given to Roosevelt, the president who
oversaw its implementation during the Great Depression
of the 1930s. According to Sanders, "FDR and his progressive coalition created the New Deal."[5] Yet this interpretation
leaves out so much that it's wrong. It misses how the New
Deal was motivated in part by the desire to "head off the
alarming growth of spontaneous rebellion in the early years
of the Roosevelt administration—organization of tenants and
the unemployed, movements of self-help, general strikes in
several cities," as historian Howard Zinn notes. "Desperate
people were not waiting for the government to help them; they
were helping themselves, acting directly."[6] Protests, sit-ins, and
other kinds of direct action against evictions and for welfare

and unemployment insurance were happening all over the country when Roosevelt took office. A strike wave began in 1934, with workers organizing themselves democratically and using militant tactics to win victories, including occupying company property and standing up to police violence. Without this upsurge of class struggle by employed and unemployed workers, the New Deal reforms would not have been brought in.[7]

These episodes in the history of the US are just two examples of how collective action by large numbers of ordinary people has forced governments to bring in major reforms that they would not have implemented otherwise. Sometimes, as in these two cases, government action has been a direct response to popular militancy. At other times the influence has been more indirect. In Sweden in the 1940s, working-class militancy led union and social democratic leaders to "adopt a radical postwar program." In office, the social democratic party brought in reforms that "laid the basis for the welfare state" for which Sweden became famous.[8] In 1943 a British Conservative MP said, "If you do not give the people reform, they are going to give you revolution,"[9] and Britain is not the only country in which rulers have been pushed to bring in reforms because they feared the consequences of not doing so. That sentiment has animated many a change in policy. Instilling it in the minds of our rulers is the only hope we have of winning progress toward a just transition. Mass social movements are what can put that fear in their minds.

What's in a Movement?
This book opened with Naomi Klein's line "Only mass social movements can save us now," so we need to be clear about what a mass social movement is. This is especially important for people who've never experienced anything like one; not knowing what one is can lead to mistaking other things for a mass social movement. Using the term "movement" to

refer to mere organizations, as lots of people do, only adds to the confusion. It's even worse when the organization is bureaucratic, with formal rules that limit what members can do and that are difficult for them to change. For example, some people involved with the Canadian Federation of Students, an organization of university and college student unions, many of which rarely or never hold general assemblies open to all their dues-paying nominal members, call it a movement. It's common to talk about a "labor movement." Bureaucratic unions made up of large numbers of workers are significant organizations, but they're not a mass social movement.

The essence of a mass social movement is large numbers of people acting together. The revolutionary socialist Leon Trotsky once wrote that "the most indubitable feature of a revolution is the direct interference of the masses in historic events." If in a revolution the masses at least "create by their own interference the initial groundwork for a new regime," a mass social movement that doesn't go that far is still people directly intervening to change society.[10] The historical examples I've mentioned demonstrate that. Revolutions involve mass social movements rising to such heights that they threaten the existing state or even the basic structure of power in society.

A social movement involves people acting together. It's all about *collective* action, not just individual choices. In a movement, what people do goes beyond the official channels of politics, such as voting in elections, and is usually disruptive. Acting together involves *organizing*.[11] This doesn't necessarily mean formal organizations structured by rules of some kind, although they're usually part of a movement. Organization is frequently informal, as in a group of neighbors who get together to protest against racist policing. For a social movement to develop, the collective action has to be *sustained*. A couple of days of protests don't make a movement, no matter how many people take part. But days of protest can give rise to a movement, and social movements often mobilize people for protest actions. There's an important link here: Organizing of some kind is needed in order for people to sustain collective action for more than brief periods of time.

A social movement becomes a mass movement when the number of participants hits a sizeable threshold for that society. A true sign that a movement is developing a mass character is that it's not just mobilizing many people but also people from many sectors of the population. Such breadth is a sign that the movement has developed a strong political magnetism, allowing it to attract people who've never taken part in contentious collective action before. This social breadth means there will inevitably be political diversity. In other words, there is always debate among people taking part in a mass movement about what exactly their goals are, what they should do to achieve them, and who are their friends and enemies.

In the spring and summer of 2020, a brief mass social movement against racism, especially racist policing, swept the US, along with solidarity protests worldwide. Sparked by the murder of George Floyd in Minneapolis—a racist police killing like so many that preceded his—people took to the streets in hundreds of cities and towns in spite of the raging COVID-19 pandemic. They took part in protests and in some cases attacked property or occupied public spaces in what can fairly be called uprisings. As one writer has observed, it began as "open black revolt: simultaneous but uncoordinated, a vivid fixture of American history sprung to life with startling speed." But "what emerged under the banner of blackness was soon blended with other elements, flinging multi-racial crowds against soldiers and police."[12] Estimates of the number of people who participated in some way between late May and early July range from fifteen to twenty-six million.[13] While led by Black people, who were disproportionately affected by both police racism and COVID-19, this was very much a movement of the multiracial working class in the US that also drew in some middle-class people. The groundwork for what took place had to some extent been laid by organizing since 2014 under the banner of Black Lives Matter, but the mass movement of 2020 was not the outcome of conscious planning by any organization.

In this it differed to some extent from another mass social movement in North America in the twenty-first century, the protests and resistance in Quebec in 2012 against tuition increases and later against the law brought in to quell the protests. This movement grew out of—but went well beyond—systematic organizing by student unions. Sometimes called the "Red Square" movement because of the symbol used by its supporters, well over three hundred thousand people out of around eight million Quebecois took part in the student strikes, marches, occupations, and other forms of collective action that went on for months. After students rejected a deal to end their strike that had been negotiated between the government and student union leaders, the government passed a law that restricted picketing and banned demonstrations of more than fifty people that had not been granted police approval. Far from quelling the movement, this draconian move further broadened it, drawing in many working-class people angered by state repression and sympathetic to the anti-neoliberal political message coming from many striking students. The governing party was forced to call an election, which it lost, leading to the cancellation of the proposed tuition hike.

Even when they erupt unexpectedly, social movements don't come out of nowhere. They don't just happen. They always involve at least some elements of conscious organizing. Even the most spontaneous-seeming movement is fed by some kind of organizing—people working to bring others together for action—although the organizing may be informal and underground, invisible to authorities and outside observers, unknown even to many people who get involved in the movement. Small-scale organizing may go on for years before circumstances change and a movement begins to take shape. Still, even tireless efforts by capable organizers aren't enough to make a movement happen, or to turn a movement into a mass movement. Most organizing efforts don't grow into movements. For that to happen there also has to be a widespread openness to action among the people that organizers are trying to persuade to act. We can see this in how in Quebec in 2015 some radical students who had taken part in the 2012 movement tried to use student strikes to spark working-class revolt against the provincial government's austerity measures. They failed. As two perceptive organizers pointed out in their assessment of the effort, "Many people didn't know about the dangers of austerity, or simply its definition and what it means. It is difficult to successfully skip the slow, laborious steps of popular education and base-building in a mass mobilization process."[14]

The Crux of the Matter

Why do mass movements matter so much at this time in history? First, they are crucial for defensive battles. Capitalism is subjecting us to continual efforts by employers and governments to chip away at what remains of past gains embedded in unions' collective agreements, public services, social programs, labor laws, and other forms of protection from the capitalist principle of "work or starve." Capitalism's irrational logic of profit also leads to more fossil fuel projects and other forms of ecological destruction. Accompanying these attacks are escalating moves against migrants, people who experience racism, and other groups of people who face oppression. Mass protest and resistance can stop such attacks. That's what happened in Quebec in 2012. In 2019 US air transport workers calling in sick and the threat of strikes pushed Trump to end his shutdown of the federal government that had left its workers without pay. When resistance isn't strong enough to stop an attack it can sometimes weaken the blow—as the protests at airports against Trump's anti-Muslim travel ban did in 2017[15]—or delay it, as many campaigns against extraction projects, such as those by Indigenous land defenders and their supporters, have been able to do. Defensive battles matter. They can keep people's lives from getting worse. They're also important because the experience of defensive fights can change those who take part in them. By boosting confidence, developing understanding and organizing skills, and strengthening relationships, they can better prepare people for future struggles. Determined resistance by a mass movement, especially when it achieves even small victories, can also give people hope that collective action can make a difference. Hope is precious. It sustains people through hard times and keeps them from turning their backs on what's going on in society and retreating into their personal lives. People with hope are also more likely to take part in future battles.

Second, only mass social movements have the power to win measures for a just transition and other reforms that challenge the priority of profit. Only mass social movements could force reluctant governments to do the previously unthinkable or push governments committed to a radical GND to go forward in spite of furious opposition from capitalists. The Red Nation, a mostly Indigenous socialist group in the US, puts it this way: "Our leverage is people. Leverage comes from a movement behind you. Only when people move do we build enough power to force concessions and eventually win."[16] As we saw in the last chapter, the capitalist class wields enormous influence on the state. Moreover, capitalist states are not neutral instruments. Green left governments cannot easily use them to enact the kind of changes needed to slash greenhouse gas emissions, improve the quality of life for the majority of people, and leave no one behind in a just transition that in settler-colonial societies like the US and Canada would need to be accompanied by a transformation in the relationship between Indigenous and non-Indigenous peoples. To overcome opposition from both corporate owners and the upper echelons of state officialdom will take a lot of power. The convergence of different forces around climate justice demands—reducing emissions, reversing austerity, rejecting oppression—has the potential to bring that much power to bear. Much as it was the self-activity of slaves that drove Lincoln to abolish slavery without compensating slave owners, as the planet heats it will take disruptive mass upsurges to bring about anything worth calling a radical GND. If a government starts to implement such climate justice reforms, movement forces will still need to maintain their independence from the state, organizing people to monitor the government's actions and spur it to stay on track and go further.

Underestimating Elections?

One challenge to this argument that mass social movements are the key to the possibility of winning a just transition is that it underestimates the importance of political parties and electoral politics. Some on the left argue that only the state has the authority and the resources to bring about a just transition. In addition, they claim that most citizens see elections as the only or at least the most legitimate way of making change in society. Some also believe that mass social movements of the kind I've been arguing are so important are unlikely to happen in time. On this basis, they contend that supporters of climate justice should focus on electing parties and leaders pledged to a green left agenda, such as Sanders in the US and the Labour Party in the UK (which even when Labour left stalwart Jeremy Corbyn was its leader was "an electoral party only," not a party that built movements as well as running candidates, as a disappointed radical Labour activist observed[17]), or work inside parties that they believe can be won to such an agenda, like the New Democratic Party in Canada. Supporters of this outlook often make their case by arguing that what's needed are green leftists in office backed and nudged by social movements. For example, Varshini Prakash of the Sunrise Movement in the US maintains, "Our aim must be *governing power*. Not just the president, not just Congress, not just statehouses and city halls across the country, but all of the above, plus independent social movements to keep pushing the envelope and hold officials accountable."[18]

People who make this case are not wrong to stress the importance of state power, and especially its central or federal level. A just transition could not be carried out on a piecemeal basis by lower-level governments and local community initiatives alone; it would take a lot of planning and resources backed up with the highest level of political authority to shift to a new energy system, phase out fossil fuels, transform transportation, renovate buildings, and so on in a way that leaves no one behind.

But to think that what matters most is who's in government or that the goal of the climate justice movement should be "governing power" makes the mistake of confusing being in office with being in power—a mistake that's literally been fatal in the history of the left, as when Chile's Popular Unity government led by Salvador Allende was overthrown by a military coup in 1973. The power of the capitalist class and the capitalist character of states themselves are major obstacles to the far-reaching reforms that are needed. No elected government could conjure away those obstacles, even if it were really dedicated to a just transition and clearly had majority support among citizens and in the legislature. To weaken those political obstacles sufficiently that a government could get a just transition underway would take massive pressure of the kind that only movements can unleash. Thus the movement's aim should be to develop the power to force governments to enact the climate justice measures that are needed. This is altogether different from seeking "governing power," a stance that treats getting "friendly" politicians into office as primary and social movements as secondary while making the mistake of thinking that being in office is the same as holding power. The more a movement limits itself to "pushing the envelope" in the sense of holding government accountable, the less it can act independently to apply the kind of relentless and escalating pressure needed to make a government act for climate justice in the face of opposition from business and top state officials.

The idea that the legitimacy of elections in the eyes of citizens means that social movements can't be the centerpiece of a strategy for change doesn't take into account declining voter turnout and other signs of disaffection with official politics. Anthropologist Alain Bertho suggests that "across the world we are seeing the official establishment of a divorce between peoples and the powers that rule over them, whatever the nature of the states concerned."[19] This tendency is a feature of capitalist society today. Failure to address the reality and looming threats of climate change is one of the reasons why the established parties and electoral politics seem increasingly irrelevant to many people.

This doesn't mean that supporters of climate justice should ignore elections, but how to relate to elections is a secondary issue. What's really at stake in this challenge is whether mass social movements are *by far the most important* ingredient for making the kind of change that's called for. Even if the odds of such movements arising and doing what needs to be done in time may not be good, it remains true that what needs to be done simply cannot be done without mass social movements.

Trusting the Sheeple?

The crucial role of mass social movements is also questioned from a different direction. There are people who believe that such movements cannot happen in rich countries (or, for some critics, anywhere) and so devastating ecological crisis and the collapse of civilization are inevitable. They conclude that it is too late to do anything but prepare for the coming collapse (an approach some call "deep adaptation"[20]) and that there is no point in movement organizing. This is what ecological writer Gabriel Levy, in an excellent critique that shows why supporters of this outlook misunderstand how ecological crisis affects societies and are wrong about how to respond to the deepening crisis, calls "disaster environmentalism."[21] Its exponents sometimes buttress their despair with laments about how most people are "sheeple" who won't mobilize for climate action or social justice. A typical example is writer Paul Kingsnorth. Looking back at his activist past, he has written, "I was an idiot. . . . Humans like ease, material comfort, entertainment and conformity, and they do not like anyone who threatens to take these things away." Now, he adds, "I live on a smallholding and grow my own food."[22] A clearer abdication of responsibility and turning away from collective action to change society would be hard to find. As I will argue in the next chapter, collective action for societal change will still be essential even if GHG emissions reach levels that guarantee warming of over 2° above preindustrial levels at some future time. Apparently "nonpolitical" counsels of despair are quite compatible with bouts of reactionary politics. Kingsnorth himself is a cautionary tale: he has written sympathetically about right-wing populism and mused, "What might a benevolent green nationalism sound like?"[23]

From another angle, there are leftists who argue that the best response to ecological crisis or capitalism more generally will come from the actions of a highly committed small minority itself, not efforts directed toward building mass movements. Today some of these people identify as insurrectionists. Whatever the label, they call for attacks by small groups of radicals on corporate or state targets. Some advocate forming clandestine cells and using guerrilla tactics of armed struggle. For such radicals, philosopher Stephen D'Arcy argues,

> most members of the general public are not seen as a potential force for radical change, to be organized by a painstaking process of movement-building in which they are won over to a transformative, antisystemic political project. Instead, they are best understood as a tool of reactionary politics—bought off by the system, and now so thoroughly incorporated into it, by means of a combination of affluence, consumerism and mass deception by the media that they are actually part and parcel of the system to be opposed.[24]

Such elitist radicals rightly scorn the idea that ruling classes will accept a just transition just because a green left government is elected or because enough people get arrested doing civil disobedience to win widespread sympathy for the moral righteousness of their cause. But their spurning of mass movements is deeply mistaken. Attacks by small groups won't win urgently needed climate justice reforms, although they will lead to more intense state repression that will hamper movement-building work. Fortunately, elitist radicalism is a significant political force in only a few countries today. Even if that were to change, as it may, this approach is a dead end for people who want to move toward a better, freer society because it fails to understand the transformative potential of social movements. D'Arcy eloquently explains that it's by engaging in collective action that people

> not only begin to change the world; they also begin to change themselves. They begin to see the potential power of collective action, to see connections between capitalism and racism or sexism or imperialism that they may not previously have grasped, and they begin to contemplate more and more far-reaching social

transformations as they gain deeper insight into the systemic roots of the social problems they hope to remedy through social action. This process of politicization, sometimes leading to radicalization, may take some time, and different people will draw different political conclusions—some more radical, some more reformist—from their experiences in struggle. But according to advocates of self-emancipation politics, there is no viable alternative to the difficult learning process in which social movements, based on self-organization of exploited and oppressed people, serve as spaces of mediation or bridge-building between millions of people and the transformative agenda of radical politics.[25]

In short, mass movements are essential because of how participating in them changes people and because of their power to repel attacks, win reforms, and open up possibilities for more far-reaching societal change; in fact, these two dimensions of mass movements are connected.

Mass Movement Climate Justice Politics

The unique power of mass social movements means that people who want to see *at least* the emergency measures needed to launch a just transition should unite around climate justice politics that focus our energies on movement building. We can practice these politics anywhere and everywhere that people are resisting or fighting for change, not just in organizing whose starting point is climate change. Moreover, we need to promote the convergence of different forces around these politics. As Klein argues, "It is the only way to build a counterpower sufficiently robust to win against the forces protecting the highly profitable but increasingly untenable status quo. Climate change acts as an accelerant to many of our social ills—inequality, wars, racism—but it can also be an accelerant for the opposite, for the forces working for economic and social justice and against militarism."[26] Because the obstacles to governments in capitalist states implementing the sweeping reforms that are needed are so large, climate justice politics should be fundamentally extraparliamentary. That is, they should be geared to organizing people in workplaces, neighborhoods, and elsewhere for mass direct action. An extraparliamentary strategic approach doesn't mean ignoring elections but approaches them from the perspective of trying to take advantage of every opportunity to build movements.

There is no denying that because there are few dynamic, growing social movements in rich countries today,[27] many people who find these politics attractive aren't sure if they're viable and worthy of their commitment. My brief response to this is threefold. First, because these are the only politics that could lead to what's urgently needed we should do our best to put them into practice. Second, recent movements and struggles give us good reason to think that mass social movements in these countries are indeed possible in our time. These include the mobilization of Indigenous people against the Dakota Access Pipeline in the US; the international movement of young students in school strikes for climate action, which at times drew in in older people; direct action by Extinction Rebellion (XR) in the UK and other militant climate groups elsewhere; women's strikes in a number of countries in Europe and South America; the *gilets jaunes* movement in France in 2018–19 and the mass strikes and protests in defense of public pensions in 2019–20; the wave of strikes by teachers and other education workers in the US in 2018–19; and the Black-led multiracial mass movement against racism in the US in 2020. Third, the terrible path that capitalism has us on will create conditions in society out of which larger social movements are more likely to erupt in the years ahead, in ways we can't predict.

It's right for people who embrace these politics to want to think about how to act on them. Yet there are no recipes for building mass social movements and winning victories.

XR's leaders claim to have one, though: openly organized, nonviolent civil disobedience by large numbers of people.[28] This, they claim, will pressure governments to eventually come to the negotiating table. XR leaders repeat the mistaken claim that 3.5 percent of the population getting actively involved in a campaign of nonviolent civil resistance in a country's capital city virtually guarantees success. They also believe that getting enough people arrested in acts of disruptive civil disobedience will lead to that magic threshold. Yet "the real power of mass civil disobedience is not its power to shock the powerful into listening to the movement, but rather its potential to draw into action the masses of people that the powerful rely on to keep businesses running."[29] Sadly, as the editors of the journal *Salvage* argue, "the strategic concept of a handful of activists trying to engineer a rebellion encompassing 3.5 per cent of the population, based as it is on a numerical abstraction of complex processes, is extreme, vainglorious voluntarism." It mistakenly assumes that activist willpower is enough to trigger an uprising. The XR strategy rests on academic research by Erica Chenoweth and Maria J. Stephan, the source of the 3.5 percent figure. However,

> their data covers exclusively campaigns for the overthrow of a government or occupying force, whether of French forces in Vietnam or Milosevic in Serbia, not the deep-going transformation of a globally organised economic and social system. Moreover, like almost all social movement theory, this research offers as explanatory *inputs* (people power, non-violence) what are in fact *outcomes*. . . . One's inquiry surely ought to be into the processes generating these outcomes . . . dense historical and political questions which are

not resoluble into a magic number, or a distilled set
of technics.[30]

Chenoweth and Stephan, whose research was intended to be
useful for US state officials, often exclude "the deeper context
of decades-long struggles, community organizing, grassroots
network building (sadly, frequently coupled with instances
of regime violence and opposition counter-violence) which
always preceded the eventual success of nonviolent strategies,"
as journalist Nafeez Ahmed points out.[31] Andreas Malm is
blunt: "Chenoweth and Stephan are not the IPCC of resistance."[32] In spite of rhetoric about building a mass movement,
in practice this XR approach substitutes self-sacrificing activists for a movement on the basis of a faulty theory of how to
make change.

Another weakness of XR's strategy is its call for governments to create unelected citizens' assemblies and then
follow their decisions about the ecological crisis. A citizens'
assembly would be made up of randomly selected persons
representative of the population of the country in question.
This idea completely ignores how the power of capitalists and
the capitalist nature of the state would be obstacles regardless
of whether a just transition were proposed by a conventional
government in the existing state or a new citizens' assembly
alongside such a government. The call for such assemblies
evades the need for mass social movements to wrest reforms
from the ruling class every step of the way, not just bring
government representatives to the table.

We shouldn't look for a ready-made, supposedly universal formula for movement-building. Instead, we should look to
where exploited and oppressed people are in motion. Whether
people are being moved to act against racism, attacks on repro-
ductive freedom, sexual violence, austerity, low pay, climate
change, or something else, wherever there is collective action
against injustice there can be potential for organizing that

aims to expand that action and build movements. Sometimes people mobilize in unexpected ways. This can present supporters of mass movement climate justice politics with the challenge of how to relate to new developments that are both promising and have the potential to head in dangerous directions.

The *gilets jaunes* protests in France in 2018–19 are a good example. A tax on diesel fuel imposed by the neoliberal government of President Emmanuel Macron triggered militant roundabout blockades, marches, and street barricades by sectors of working-class and self-employed people who generally had not been part of earlier anti-austerity mobilizations. Many of them carried French flags and sang the national anthem. Far-right forces tried to channel the protests into a revolt against taxes and immigrants that ignored or even denied the need for climate action. But a range of left-wing forces also participated in the movement. Their ongoing participation allowed previously depoliticized people to meet and work with left organizers. Sharing experiences in the movement helped leftists to challenge right-wing ideas and encourage the movement's main thrust against social inequality and for the redistribution of wealth. The experience of intense police violence also led many white participants to start to understand what non-white people in France have long known about the police and the links between racism, poverty, and repression. The slogan "*Fin du monde, fin du mois, même combat*" ("End of the world [i.e., climate change], end of the month [i.e., poverty], same struggle") exemplified climate justice politics in the movement. The *gilets jaunes* movement forged a powerful link between "issues of environmental disaster and climate change" and "questions of social and political justice," and this transformed ecological politics in France.[33]

Some mobilizations have more potential than others to build a powerful movement. There are a number of features that create such potential. These need to be fostered wherever possible. Modelling them even in very small ways is important in nurturing a culture of fighting to win. One valuable quality is an orientation to drawing in larger and larger numbers of people, reaching beyond the ranks of those who've participated in previous protests. When this starts to happen, there's always the risk that people with more experience of climate justice politics will be dismissive of those who are only beginning to demand action. Socialist academic Keeanga-Yamahtta Taylor's response to how some on the left responded to the January 2017 Women's March in the US is relevant here:

> Liberals become radicals through their own frustrating experiences with the system, but also through becoming engaged with people who became radical before them. So when radicals who have already come to some important conclusions about the shortcomings of existing systems mock, deride or dismiss those who have not achieved the same level of consciousness, they are helping no one. . . . Should the marches have been more multiracial and working class? Yes! But you are not a serious organizer if that's where your answer to the question ends. The issue for the left is how we get from where we are today to where we want to be in terms of making our marches blacker, browner and more working class. Simply complaining about it changes nothing.[34]

Another important quality is drawing people into active ongoing participation in movement organizations. Instead of sending people home and telling them to wait for the next big event, people can be encouraged to get involved in groups that organize to build the movement in between large mobilizations. This is different from how NGOs generally operate, which rarely goes beyond signing people up to give money and receive information and requests to send e-mails or make phone calls to elected officials. Democratic participatory forms of organizing that put participants—not union or NGO officials, politicians, or unaccountable activist leaders—in charge of their own efforts are precious. A stance of solidarity toward other struggles is also an important quality. So too is the understanding that one mobilization is rarely enough to win.

Militant tactics that use or move toward using disruptive mass direct action are another important feature that gives a mobilization positive potential to go further. Forms of mass direct action that have an impact on corporate profits or impede the functioning of the state—for example, mass strikes by workers and large-scale blockades of transport networks used to move commodities to markets—have the most power to squeeze reforms from governments. As four US socialist supporters of a GND have written, "The working class has a 'lever' at the core of the operation of the capitalist system. If workers stop working, or go on strike, business as usual grinds to a halt. . . . When workers strike, or organize other mass disruptive actions, those in power are forced to pay attention."[35] The impact that workers have when they withdraw their labor and strike is one of the reasons why workplace organizing and unions are important for climate justice supporters, in spite of the many limits of unions as they exist today.[36] That said, workers' strikes are not the only kind of mass direct action that can be effective.

What about vandalism and sabotage? Is this a tactic that can help build a movement powerful enough to push states into a just transition? Andreas Malm, who advocates building a mass climate justice movement, calls for part of the movement to carry out targeted attacks on GHG-emitting property, from pipelines to SUVs, in ways that take great care not to injure or kill people. This would, he believes, discourage further investments in such property and show that it can be made inoperable, with the goal of compelling "states to proclaim the prohibition and begin retiring the stock."[37] Malm makes a convincing case that attacks on property are ethical. But would this tactic really help the movement achieve the goal of making states phase out fossil fuels? He quotes historian Verity Burgmann: "The history of social movement activity suggests that reforms are more likely to be achieved when activists behave in extremist, even confrontational ways. Social movements rarely achieve everything they want, but they secure important partial victories when one wing, flanking the rising tide in the mainstream, prepares to blow the status quo sky-high."[38] This point about the role of a "radical flank" of a rising mass movement is right. But it is extremely unlikely that attacks on pipelines and other fossil fuel targets by small groups of activists would be such a flank, one that could make a government decide to finally take decisive action to decarbonize society. Such attacks might hurt the profits of some firms, but they would cause little disruption to the regular functioning of capitalist society. However, they would certainly lead to more state repression against the climate movement—and not just the groups of activists working secretly to carry out vandalism and sabotage. This would make it more difficult to organize effective kinds of mass direct action like strikes, occupations, blockades, and incursions that disrupt fossil fuel extraction or distribution, such as the 2016 Ende Gelände anti-coal mass actions in Germany that Malm rightly praises. There is also the problem that the more damage is done by attacks on property, the more spectacular they are. As Trotsky observed, "The more the attention of the masses is focused on them—the more they reduce the interest of the masses in self-organization and self-education."[39] In addition, people engaged in campaigns of sabotage have to operate in small clandestine groups to avoid arrest, often withdrawing from other movement activity. Activists operating that way are at risk of treating what they're doing as a substitute for mass movement building, falling into the kind of elitist radicalism criticized earlier in this chapter. For these reasons people who want to build a mass climate justice movement should reject the tactic of attacks on property by small groups or lone individuals.[40]

No matter what the immediate issue is, supporters of mass movement climate justice politics can become constructive participants in people's struggles and help to build them using these politics. If people aren't already in motion, we can work patiently with others to turn discontent about injustice into collective action for change. This will often mean taking part in community and workplace organizing whose focus is not climate change, for understandable reasons: All over the world there are many immediate problems, all manner of affronts to human dignity, that today affect people more than climate shifts. This means that climate justice politics must be "trans-environmental," as philosopher Nancy Fraser puts it.[41] Fortunately, it's possible for supporters of climate justice to participate in a mobilization about other issues and, over time, promote convergences among movements and persuade more people of the importance of striving for a just transition. The *gilets jaunes* experience in France demonstrates this. Understanding that capitalism—always interwoven with many forms of oppression—is the underlying cause of the ecological crisis *and* of so much social injustice can help organizers to link struggles and forge solidarity across the real differences that divide exploited and oppressed people. "An injury to one is an injury to all" is an old working-class movement slogan worth reclaiming and acting on. So too is a saying that emerged from Indigenous activism in Australia in the 1970s: "If you have come here to help me, you are wasting your time. But if you have come because your liberation is bound up with mine, then let us work together."

4.

"Even a Ravaged Planet Is Worth Fighting For"

So far this book has attempted to answer the question of how best to work for what's needed: slashing GHG emissions on the scale and timeline indicated by climate science and in a way that tackles social injustice and leaves no one behind.[1] That is the question thrown up by climate justice organizing globally. We should do everything possible to attain this goal. At the same time, however, we need to confront the terrible truth that GHG emissions may well reach levels that will lead to future warming above 2°, with devastating consequences on a large scale, and to think about the political implications of this possibility.

2030 or Bust?

It's not uncommon to hear people say that we have until 2030 (the year the Intergovernmental Panel on Climate Change set as a deadline in its well-known 2018 report) to drastically cut emissions or "it's game over, folks," as one climate activist in Canada put it.[2] This sense of urgency is extremely important. There is nothing wrong with the intentions of people who say such things or carry placards at demonstrations with that message. That said, there are problems with such all-or-nothing thinking about cutting emissions.

One problem is that if more than a few climate scientists reach the conclusion that emissions levels make future warming of over 2° inevitable or close to inevitable people who believe that this means the end of the world will experience intense mental distress. The emotional impact of thinking about what climate change is doing and could do in the future to the lives of many millions of people is already causing a lot of distress, which will only increase as the planet heats up. This misery is a burden for the people who experience it. It also makes it harder for them to take part in collective action for climate justice, which is becoming all the more important and can also help us cope with distress connected to awareness of climate change.

Another problem is that all-or-nothing thinking about emissions can lead people to support climate politics that offer little or no challenge to social injustice. It's not only denial about the need for action or ineffective policy proposals that should concern climate justice supporters. There are also political responses that aim to quickly reduce emissions in drastic ways but that don't respect the principles of climate justice. If global GHG emission levels continue to make heating over 2° probable, more people are likely to endorse urgent calls for deep emissions cuts that aren't linked to social justice if those calls seem the most realistic or politically acceptable response. For example, there may be more moves to slash emissions that aren't accompanied by commitments to create decent jobs for workers whose jobs will be eliminated in the transition from fossil fuels. Or there may be plans to expand nuclear power generation, whose ecological and social consequences should rule it out for supporters of climate justice.[3] Policies could be proposed that would bring about a speedy transition from fossil energy but reduce funding for public services and raise taxes in regressive ways to pay for it. Desperation could drive people to form underground cells to carry out sabotage or, worse, assassination attempts on government figures or executives of fossil fuel firms.

Even worse is the prospect of support for a multinational scheme to reduce global emissions and construct a system of solar radiation management (SRM) to lower temperatures.

SRM is a kind of geoengineering that would inject synthetic aerosols into Earth's atmosphere in order to reflect more sunlight and cool the planet. Once established, SRM would have to be maintained far into the future; interrupting the aerosol injections would trigger devastating warming. For such a scheme to be effective, there would have to be some kind of multinational institution with the ability to oversee it. As Joel Wainwright and Geoff Mann argue, that institution could make "decisions over the fate of the Earth's climate and energy, nothing less than life and death."[4] This would require backup from decisive power—ultimately, military might—over the world to enforce the rules of the SRM scheme.

Less frightening proposals could still be easily tied to suspending civil and democratic rights, flowing with today's trend toward "minimalist democracy" in which, in the words of Richard Seymour, "the ideal form of democratic account-ability . . . is the single-issue plebiscite, and the celebrity election."[5] It is not hard to imagine politicians arguing that the climate emergency justifies not only bold state action to transition from fossil fuels but also forcibly relocating people from coastal areas, further restricting cross-border migra-tion, banning strikes, or overriding the rights of Indigenous peoples. An endless range of reactionary policies could be justified in the name of saving Earth. All-or-nothing thinking about cutting GHG emissions encourages acceptance of such policies.

Quite simply, the world won't end if we learn that future warming over 2° has become inevitable, with the prospect of feedbacks further accelerating climate change. It won't be "game over" for the billions of people alive at the time. Instead we would find ourselves facing an even more fright-ening future. The need for a "comprehensive reorganization of human societies in the reasonably near term" would become even clearer than it is today, but "*who* will survive, and *how* they will live" would be even more of a question.[6]

If we find ourselves in this situation, it will be even more important than it is now to struggle for a just transition from fossil fuels and other sources of GHG emissions. The difference between a world with an average temperature 2.5° higher than preindustrial levels in 2100 and still warming and one that's 3.5° hotter and warming even faster—"the difference between historically unprecedented suffering and full-on apocalypse"—will be measured in millions of deaths.[7] The struggle over how societies adapt to climate change—the fight for what we can call *just adaptation*—will also grow in importance as the climate scenario worsens. Malm is right: "Overshoot of targets for climate mitigation calls for more, not less, resistance . . . as long as humans are around, resistance is the path to survival in all weathers; it didn't become passé in 2009 and it won't do so in 2029."[8]

Our Rulers' Responses

It's understandable that some people refuse to think about frightening future developments that may well happen. While it's not helpful to dwell too much on such matters—the pressing tasks of organizing today demand our attention, along with awareness of other dimensions of our everyday lives in the present—it's also unwise to avoid some consideration of what we're likely to encounter if it becomes clear that it is no longer possible to avoid a future with warming of over 2°.

I will avoid specific predictions; as argued earlier, there are different possible political responses to climate change. It is these that will shape the social arrangements that will determine how people will be affected in different parts of the world. However, we should recognize that there are ruling-class intellectuals who are thinking about the future of the social order in a world of worsening climate impacts. Whether they are employed by state agencies, universities, think tanks, or other institutions, their outlook is not limited to next quarter's profits or winning the next election. They will start to cultivate support for schemes to mitigate climate change and adapt to it in ways designed to ensure that social order will be maintained and profits made. In imperialist countries including the US, Canada, the UK, and China, we can expect that these schemes will also be concerned with preserving the country's place in the hierarchical global system of states. In such countries we can also expect proposals to be no more concerned about the lives of the majority of humanity that dwells in the imperialized regions of the world than those states' policies are today. Given the scale of the climate crisis, they'll probably show even less concern for the global majority. As Naomi Klein writes, "A culture that places so little value on black and brown lives that it is willing to let human beings disappear beneath the waves, or set themselves on fire in detention centres, will also be willing to let the countries where black and brown people live disappear beneath the waves, or desiccate in the arid heat. When that happens, theories of human hierarchy—that we must take care of our own first—will be marshalled to rationalise these monstrous decisions."[9]

Everywhere we can expect ruling-class adaptation and mitigation schemes will make a disproportionate share of the costs fall to those who are not rich and powerful. SRM is likely to be part of more policy packages. We should expect to see responses animated by the "never let a serious crisis go to waste" spirit that treated the aftermath of the Great Recession of 2008–9 as an opportunity to advance neoliberal proposals, which were presented to citizens as necessary to combat swelling deficits and debt. The details will reflect the conditions of capitalism at the time, but the objective will be to boost the profits and power of the dominant class and the authority of states in a warming world.

Most predictions about what will happen if climate change starts to severely affect advanced capitalist countries aren't worth much because they are informed by flimsy analysis. But what climate justice organizer Jonathan Neale writes deserves to be taken seriously because it's based on a strong understanding of how these societies work:

> When the moment of runaway climate change comes for you, where you live, it will not come in the form of a few wandering hairy bikers. It will come with the tanks on the streets and the military or the fascists taking power. Those generals will talk in deep green language. They will speak of degrowth, and the boundaries of planetary ecology. They will tell us we have consumed too much, and been too greedy, and now for the sake of Mother Earth, we must tighten our belts. Then we will tighten our belts, and we will suffer, and they will build a new kind of gross green inequality. And in a world of ecological freefall, it will take cruelty on an unprecedented scale to keep their inequality in place.[10]

It's that kind of outcome that supporters of climate justice must be prepared to fight to prevent—or overturn.

Keeping On in Catastrophic Times

If capitalism makes extremely dangerous, rather than simply dangerous, climate change inevitable, powerful mass social movements will become even more vital. They would have to struggle for just adaptation, with proactive measures to prepare for foreseeable disasters, and a just transition. At the same time they would need to lead resistance to reactionary adaptation and mitigation policies. Movements would also have to defend whatever remains of democracy and civil liberties in capitalist democracies against attempts to further restrict or suspend them altogether, which would likely be justified in the name of dealing with the climate emergency. Movement organizers would need to counter such moves with bold proposals to expand and deepen democracy. These could include the democratic planning and implementation of just adaptation and transition measures by people in their communities and workplaces. The principled political commitments that are needed today would become even more important. These include welcoming migrants in a spirit of egalitarian hospitality and internationalist opposition to borders, genuine international assistance by rich countries for poorer ones in a spirit of anti-imperialism, and consistent opposition to racism and settler colonialism. Movements would need to fight for measures that make capitalists pay for the crises their system has brought about, rather than having the burden inflicted on the dispossessed majority that doesn't own or control the means of producing goods and services. These reforms could include sharply progressive taxes on profits, savings, and income as well as the expropriation of wealth.

Malm has noted that during the First World War the Russian revolutionary socialist V.I. Lenin "spoke of the catastrophe of his time as a 'mighty accelerator' bringing all contradictions to a head, 'engendering world-wide crises of unparalleled intensity,' driving nations 'to the brink of doom.'" Malm perceptively suggests that "climate change is likely to be the accelerator of the twenty-first century, speeding up the contradictions of late capitalism—above all the growing chasm between the evergreen lawns of the rich and the precariousness of propertyless existence—and expedite one local catastrophe after another." This will probably lead to murderously repressive efforts to maintain the unequal status quo. But profound social crises can also lead to the beginnings of revolution when large numbers of people conclude that conventional politics don't allow them to deal with the problems convulsing society. As Malm puts it, "revolution to *treat* the symptoms of global warming" is possible. This could grow into people starting to uproot the causes of socioecological crisis and launch a transition in the direction of a society in which climate justice could be fully realized—the topic of the next chapter. "If social relations block the way to effective pro-poor adaptation, they ought to be overhauled. Here is one more reason to seize every opportunity catastrophes open up."[11] The Out of the Woods Collective puts it this way: "We cannot adopt the perverse fatalism of 'the worse, the better' [or] wait for some final hurricane to blow away the old order. Rather . . . even the largest scale and most terrifying of these extraordinary disasters can interrupt the ordinary disaster that is, most of the time, too large to fully comprehend. These are moments of interruption that, while horrific for human life, might also spell disaster *for* capitalism."[12] Here it is worth mentioning writer Rebecca Solnit's finding, after researching a number of twentieth-century disasters, that, contrary to what the mainstream media depicts and what rulers fear about how people behave when disasters happen, "there are plural and contingent natures—but the prevalent human nature in disaster is resilient, resourceful, generous, empathic, and brave."[13]

If revolutionary situations develop, supporters of climate justice ought to take advantage of them and strive for mass movements to make their outcomes revolutionary-democratic change. When a revolutionary situation develops, the stakes are high: historical experience shows that such crises often end with counter-revolutionary repression that smothers the possibility of change from below with a great deal of bloody violence. That is what happened, for example, to the 1871 Paris Commune. Following France's devastating defeat in the Franco-Prussian War, workers and artisans took control of its largest city and ran it through their own radically democratic institutions for just over two months, until they were crushed by the army.[14] More recently, the last embers of the Egyptian Revolution, whose accomplishments were nowhere near as radical as those of the Paris Commune, were extinguished by a military coup in 2013.

Above all, no matter how severe climate change becomes, supporters of climate justice will have an ethical responsibility to continue to struggle, regardless of how frightened we are and how difficult our circumstances. Neale is blunt: "I know why people want to go off the grid, run for the hills, live in bioregional communities. But they are so wrong. They abandon the people of Khartoum, Shanghai, the Mekong Delta, Birmingham, London, New York, New Orleans, Mumbai, Kolkota. Shame on them."[15] "The severity of the situation shouldn't undermine the willingness to act," is how Indigenous historian and socialist organizer Nick Estes puts it. "Not to act, to succumb to a kind of paralysis, of inaction, is itself an action. Not doing anything is doing something."[16]

At root, we have this responsibility because as long as there are humans on this planet, it matters what their social conditions are. That's why even a ravaged planet is worth fighting for. Our social conditions are critical because they have so much influence on the quality of our lives, which is what really matters. As philosopher Jeff Noonan contends, "Life is of ultimate value *just because* it is finite, mortal, embodied, terrestrial, of contingent origins, always fragile, and thus a necessary object of care and concern."[17] Our ethical compass should maintain and enhance the quality of life in even the most dire circumstances. This compels us to act collectively for change, no matter the odds. As ecosocialist researcher and activist Thea Riofrancos has written, "The opposite of pessimism isn't self-assured optimism, but rather militant commitment to collective action in the face of uncertainty and danger."[18] Rosie Warren, lead editor of the journal *Salvage*, puts it well: "We do not, and should not, do the things we do because we are certain we will win. We can never be certain. We do them—should do them—because we cannot do anything other."[19] In a similar vein, in *Hope without Optimism*—a fitting outlook for our times—theorist Terry Eagleton invites us to consider that "it is irrational to hope for the impossible, but not for the vastly improbable." True, "there may be no hope; but unless we act as though there is, that possibility is likely to become a certainty."[20]

Sources of Sustenance

There are many histories from which supporters of climate justice can learn and draw inspiration to help sustain ourselves today and in the more difficult, chaotic times ahead. These include the postapocalyptic resistance and free-dom struggles of Indigenous peoples. A caution is essential: Indigenous experiences of oppression under settler coloni-alism are unique. They are fundamentally unlike anything non-Indigenous people in advanced capitalist countries will ever undergo. Settler-colonial oppression is also substantially different from other forms of imperialist domination and occupation. (There are more similarities with extreme forms of racial oppression, like the Nazi attempt to exterminate the Jewish population of Europe.) The genocidal violence of settler colonialism is not like the killing or callous indifference to life that capitalist states mete out to the non-Indigenous poor, migrants, and other targets. Settler colonialism dispossesses Indigenous people in order to take control of their lands. In the US, Canada, Australia, and elsewhere, it has attempted to eliminate Indigenous people, culturally and sometimes physi-cally.[21] Once we recognize the difference between this kind of oppression and what capitalism does to the rest of us, non-In-digenous people can still learn from how Indigenous people have survived, resisted, and fought for freedom. Estes, talking about Indigenous people in North America, puts it this way:

> Indigenous people are post-apocalyptic. In some cases, we have undergone several apocalypses. . . . I don't want to universalize that experience; it was very unique to us as nations. But if there is something you can learn from Indigenous people, it's what it's like to live in a post-apocalyptic society. . . . In times of great turmoil and destruction, people didn't just stop being humans. They didn't just give up. . . . They did their best to keep alive the nation through genocide.[22]

Those of us who are not survivors of settler-colonial genocide may still learn from what Estes calls "the long tradition of Indigenous resistance."[23]

The experiences of the Palestinians, an Indigenous nation in another part of the world, are also relevant. Malm, who has spent time in Palestine in addition to fighting for climate justice in Europe, writes in a brilliant essay that "Palestinian politics is always already post-apocalyptic: it is about surviving after the end of the world and, in the best case, salvaging something out of all that has been lost." "Palestine," he suggests, "provides a human vantage point for seeing the truth about capitalist modernity known to most non-human life forms. It's just one damn *nakba* [catastrophe] after another." There are direct parallels to what climate change under capitalism will mean: "Millions will have to move along the Palestinian axis. There will be deserts, heat, fire, smoke, debris and drowning, first for masses of fisherfolk, labourers, peasants, street vendors and mothers working in their homes, and then, if the warming proceeds unabated, for pretty much everyone else."

Malm draws our attention to the Palestinian culture of *sumud*, steadfastness, whose principles are "surviving and staying put" and "resistance." "Learning to fight—not die—and to nourish some climate *sumud*" will be how to survive in a climate change–wracked world. "Moreover, if we hold the view that Palestine and climate change are not some minor deviations from an otherwise healthy trajectory of progress, but that late capitalism is rather a fundamentally *destructive* force in society as well as in nature, then we must accept that loss is a major predicament of our time, and that many struggles will have to start from baselines strewed with rubble."[24] We will be better able to cope and fight in dark times if we can take in that understanding, digest it intellectually and emotionally, and allow it to inform our actions.

There are many other histories of resistance and struggle, often little-known, that can help sustain us in times when rational fear about what the future will be like is added to the growing everyday difficulties many of us are dealing with. Which experiences and traditions resonate strongly depends on how we see ourselves and our relationship to history. That said, some histories are particularly relevant to supporters of climate justice. If GHG emissions are not brought down enough to avert extremely dangerous climate change later this century, supporters of climate justice will face growing pressure to lower our horizons and settle for calls for action that would reduce emissions but leave injustice untouched. Similarly, the growth of hard-right and far-right political forces will put more pressure on us to support their opponents of the extreme center—such as the establishment of the Democratic Party in the US and the Liberal Party in Canada—or the tepid left that accepts neoliberalism, like the NDP in Canada, instead of building movements for far-reaching change. With these prospects in mind, past fighters for social transformation who remained committed to their vision and principles in extraordinarily difficult circumstances are especially relevant.

Among the heroic organizers who fit that description were internationalist socialists in European countries occupied by the armed forces of Nazi Germany during the Second World War. Anyone seeking inspiration from people who displayed not just courage—which was shown by everyone who actively took part in resistance to fascism—but also determination to remain true to liberatory politics instead of accepting the goal of a lesser evil will find no better example than the Revolutionary Socialist Workers Party in the Netherlands. This was a political organization of anti-Stalinist radical socialists numbering over two thousand members in 1939. Its foremost leader was Henk Sneevliet. Anticipating that Germany might invade and take over the Netherlands, prior to the war it created an underground organization, the Marx-Lenin-Luxemburg Front (MLLF). After German forces overran the country, the leaders of the Dutch Social Democratic Party

didn't try to resist while the Communist Party (CP) prevar-
icated because of the nonaggression pact between Stalin's
USSR (which the CP supported uncritically) and Hitler's
Germany. "In contrast, the MLL Front tried to develop workers' actions that combined the struggle for socialism with
the fight against fascism. The organization stayed away from
nationalist resistance groups led by right-wing figures. It also
kept its distance from other leftist groups that in their opinion didn't distance themselves from the warring countries."[25]
In February 1941, after Nazi forces responded to resistance
by starting to target the Jewish community, strikes broke out
in Amsterdam and began to spread to other cities. Members
of the larger CP played key roles in the strike, and the MLLF
participated actively. In 1942 almost all of the MLLF's leaders
were captured and executed.

The members of the MLLF were not the only socialists
in Nazi-ruled countries in Europe who shared a commitment
to opposing not just fascism but also capitalism itself—which
was the basis for the colonialism in Africa and Asia upheld
by the rulers of the Western European countries at war with
Germany, Italy, and Japan, as well as for fascism—and who
rejected the nationalism of most of the anti-Nazi resistance.
Inside occupied France, some of these socialists even produced
German-language leaflets and newspapers aimed at fomenting
dissent among ordinary members of the occupying forces.[26] In
occupied Poland, the sizeable Jewish socialist party known as
the Bund "did not suspend its activities for the shortest time,"
as onetime member Marek Edelman recalled.[27] Members of
the Bund operated underground, even within the confines of
the Warsaw Ghetto. There, cut off from the rest of the world
by German troops and living in overcrowded conditions of
terrible hunger and disease, Bund members organized mutual
aid, published no fewer than half a dozen periodicals, and
conducted educational and cultural activities. In cooperation
with other political organizations, they prepared for armed

revolt against the German occupation. When in April 1943 the Nazis moved to ship the remaining Jews in the city to extermination camps, Jewish armed units, in which the Bund was central, rose up and fought back even though they knew they could not win.

Again, the point in drawing attention to the struggles of Indigenous people in North America and Palestine and the organizing of internationalist socialists in Europe against Nazi occupation isn't to suggest that capitalism is going to put non-Indigenous people in situations that are the same as theirs were or are. It's to encourage those of us who haven't experienced what Estes calls "times of great turmoil and destruction" to appreciate how even in very dangerous and difficult conditions people have not just survived but also held on to unpopular principles and continued to fight for liberation. We and those who come after us will need to do the same.

5.

Ecosocialism

As I have argued, mass social movements are the most effective way for people to resist injustice, no matter how dire the circumstances. They are the only force with the potential to win a just transition from fossil fuels and other urgently needed social and ecological reforms. Yet these aren't the only reasons why powerful mass movements are important. They are also the key to any possibility of breaking with capitalism and starting the transition toward a self-governing society with a nondestructive relationship to the rest of nature—ecosocialism.

System Change

There should be no doubt that a break with capitalism itself is needed. The best-case scenario for climate change is that GHG emissions are cut so much that future warming is limited to 1.5° or, less unlikely, under 2° *and* that rising temperatures don't trigger large-scale feedback mechanisms. Ideally such emissions cuts would be made through a just and rapid shift away from fossil fuels and from other sources of GHG pollution, accompanied with a range of actions to draw down GHG levels in ways consistent with climate justice principles, including planting trees on a very large scale.[1] Even in that best-case situation, however, the system would still be making other dimensions of the global ecological crisis worse because of its inbuilt profit-driven rhythms or, to use a different phrase, laws of motion. Capital's inexorable drive to expand the scale and speed of production would still be disrupting the Earth System in very damaging ways. Even if we are fortunate enough to limit climate change to dangerous rather than extremely dangerous levels, we will still face worsening species extinction, ocean acidification, pandemics, and other serious ecological problems. It's with this in mind that growing numbers of climate justice supporters are rejecting capitalism altogether. The ecological writer and activist George Monbiot speaks for many of them:

> For most of my adult life I've railed against "corporate capitalism," "consumer capitalism" and "crony capitalism." It took me a long time to see that the problem is not the adjective but the noun. . . . As I've grown older, I've come to recognize . . . that it is the system, rather than any variant of the system, that drives us inexorably towards disaster. . . . Capitalism collapses without growth, yet perpetual growth on a finite planet leads inexorably to environmental calamity. . . . As the scale of economic activity increases until capitalism affects everything, from the atmosphere to the deep ocean floor, the entire planet becomes a sacrifice zone. . . . This drives us towards cataclysm on such a scale that most people have no means of imagining it.[2]

Many young climate activists are reaching the same conclusion in much less time than it took Monbiot.

Capitalism's drive to ecological calamity isn't the only reason why a new system is needed. This way of organizing society consistently subordinates the life of humanity and other species to profit. Under capitalism, people's ability to get access to what they need depends mainly on being able to pay for them. Some of these requirements are physical: healthy food, clean water, adequate clothing and shelter, safety, and health care. Others are sociocultural: caring relationships, education, nonalienated work, opportunities for people to develop their capacities and flourish. People also need free time.[3] Capitalism has created greater possibilities for meeting these needs than ever before, thanks to its competition-driven development of the technologies and forms of social cooperation that together are the productive powers of human labor. Yet capitalism systematically blocks people's ability to meet their needs and live well because of how it makes profits supreme. As a consequence, "never before have the possibilities for a good world for the human species as a whole been greater. At the same time, the gap between human potential and the existing conditions of humankind in its totality has probably never been wider," observes sociologist Göran Therborn.[4] Most of the world's population does not own or control a firm. Nor do most people belong to the well-off layers of managers, self-employed professionals, and other middle-class elements. The immense majority of people are part of the working class or the peasantry. The extent to which members of these classes and other dispossessed people are able to obtain the requirements of life owes a lot to the past struggles of social movements and to where people live in a world shaped by capitalism's highly unequal imperialist development. Today, many of the past gains of movements and popular resistance are under attack by corporations seeking higher profits and governments implementing austerity. These include public education, public health care in the places where it exists, and time to rest and enjoy life before returning to the grind of working to be able to buy commodities and doing unpaid work in the home.

Ecosocialism

What kind of alternative to capitalism is needed? Quite simply, we need a society that's organized to meet human needs while maintaining a non-ecocidal relationship with the rest of nature. In such a society the priority would be repairing the rift that capitalism has created in humanity's social metabolism—a concept that grasps "'the complex, dynamic interchange between human beings and nature' of matter and energy, which recognize[s] how both 'nature-imposed conditions' and human actions transform this process"[5]—with the rest of nature, in ways that dismantle all forms of exploitation, alienation, and oppression. In the words of ecosocialist Michael Löwy, this would be "an ecologically rational society founded on democratic control, social equality, and the predominance of use value. . . . This conception assumes collective ownership of the means of production, democratic planning that makes it possible for society to define the goals of investment and production, and a new technological structure of the productive forces."[6]

Unlike capitalism, such a way of organizing society would not be driven to expand production without limit and at an ever-accelerating pace. This would be a self-governing social order in which climate justice could be fully attained, along with liberation from all forms of oppression. More broadly, we can think of it as an ecological civilization. Far from imposing cultural uniformity, it would provide the context for a flourishing of human diversity. As the Zapatistas expressed this aspiration: "In the world we want everyone fits. In the world we want many worlds to fit."[7]

Ecosocialism could not be attained immediately after breaking with capitalism. It could only be the outcome of a long period of transformation, repair, and reconstruction. The sign that a transition toward ecosocialism was underway would be democratic economic planning starting to replace the regulation of production by capitalist markets. Decisions about what to produce, how to produce, and how to allocate goods and services to people would be planned democratically, rather than being made by capitalists locked in competition or by state managers not subject to democratic popular control. Löwy continues:

Of course many scientific and technological achievements of modernity are precious, but the whole productive system must be transformed, and this can be done only by ecosocialist methods: i.e., through a democratic planning of the economy that takes into account the preservation of the ecological equilibrium . . . democratic planning is the exercise by a whole society of its freedom of decision. This is what is required for liberation from the alienating and reified "economic laws" and "iron cages" of capitalist and bureaucratic structures.[8]

People's ability to work would no longer be a commodity sold in labor markets. Workplaces would be organized democratically, with self-management replacing the hierarchies of capitalist management. Free access to priority goods and services would be introduced. Everyone would be required to contribute to society in ways that consider individuals' abilities and disabilities. Like all important social decisions, choices about which goods and services to make available for free would be made democratically. Monbiot's phrase "private sufficiency, public luxury" conveys the spirit of the kind of social-ecological reconstruction that would be involved: enhancing quality of life by providing access to high-quality public recreation, entertainment, and transportation, not by buying more commodities.[9] In societies where capitalism had been organized through settler colonialism, it would be essential that the right to self-determination of Indigenous nations be fully recognized from the very start of the transition; it would be up to Indigenous nations to shape their social arrangements and decide their relationship to the transition to ecosocialism. In such societies there would also need to be restitution for settler colonialism; returning land to Indigenous peoples would be central to this. Key measures of progress in the transition to ecosocialism would include

the amount of free time people had, along with ways of meas-
uring ecological repair and the reconstruction of society in
ecologically rational ways. Another important indicator would
be how much the scope of democratic economic planning
had expanded, shrinking the sphere of markets. The degree
to which gender, racial, sexual, and other forms of oppression
had been eliminated would also be measures of progress.

Ecosocialism has nothing in common with the way of
organizing society that was first established in the USSR at
the end of the 1920s, replicated in the parts of Eastern Europe
that came under "Communist" rule after the Second World
War, and adopted in China, Cuba, and other countries where
"Communist" parties took power as the outcome of struggles
against Western imperialism and domestic governments
subservient to it. This is not just because of the ecological
destruction that took place as the rulers of one-party states
strove to industrialize their countries, although there is no
question that this happened on a large scale. It's because the
social order in those societies wasn't socialist or in transition to socialism of any kind, no matter what was proclaimed
in their rulers' ideology. In these bureaucratic dictatorships
production wasn't democratically planned at all, only bureau-
cratically directed from above. The goal of production wasn't
meeting human needs but the expansion of national industry.[10]

What reason is there to think that it's possible to begin
the transition from capitalism to an ecologically rational
cooperative commonwealth based on democratic economic
planning? Contrary to what capitalism's ideologues would
have us think, "Planning is not only possible, but is already all
around us, albeit in hierarchical and undemocratic forms," as
Leigh Phillips and Michal Rozworski point out in their book
on the subject.[11] The internal workings of many giant corporations, including such well-known monsters as Walmart and
Amazon, are already planned. For example, within Walmart
"the different departments, stores, trucks and suppliers do not

compete against each other in a market; everything is coordinated." This extends to many of the company's suppliers. Thanks to today's information and communication technology, vast quantities of data are continuously gathered and used to track, forecast, and shape demand as efficiently as possible. Amazon excels at this. Obviously such firms are masters of controlling and exploiting workers, and their planning doesn't take ecological rationality into account—after all, they're driven by profit. Thus "there is no machine that can simply be taken over, run by new operators but otherwise left unchanged; but there is a foundation of planning that a more just society could surely take up and make its own."[12] Today's "big data" digital feedback technology, like the kind used by Uber to set prices and by its drivers and passengers to rate each other, could be modified and put to use for ecosocialist purposes. These might include democratic economic planning, identifying new needs and how to meet them, and solving other complex problems of coordination.[13] The technological foundations of a very different society built under capitalism would need to be transformed as they were repurposed for use in a transition to ecosocialism. Above all, they would need to be democratized at all levels, from the workplace up to countrywide and ultimately international scales. But they do already exist.

How Could a Transition Begin?

What would it take to launch a transition to a self-governed, ecologically rational society? The prerequisite is political: The transfer of power in some part of the world from the ruling class of the capitalist social order to the vast majority of people whose mental and manual labor is today harnessed to capital and its states (or who are treated as worthless because their labor power is not required by employers). Getting radical green left forces to form the government within existing state institutions would not bring about this transfer of class power. As we've seen, existing states are capitalist states. Changing government may lead to reforms, but it doesn't alter which class rules. It leaves capitalists in control of most workplaces and decisions about economic activity. Nor does the formation of a radical government change the nature of the state. Its institutions of service delivery, economic and social management, policing, punishment, war, and surveillance remain insulated from democratic control by the population. Forming a radical green left government in a capitalist state may well happen as part of the process that leads to a transfer of power from the capitalist class to the working class (which, let's recall, encompasses everyone who is forced to sell their ability to work in exchange for pay and has little or no management authority, along with most unwaged people) and other nonexploiters.[14] However, forming a radical government alone wouldn't be enough to start a transition beyond capitalism. That would require the creation of new highly democratic institutions through which the vast majority of people can govern themselves in all spheres of society, and for these institutions to replace those of the existing state.[15] Within those new forms of popular power, ecosocialists would have to democratically win majority support for the kind of reconstruction necessary to initiate social-ecological transformation. The seeds of such new democratic institutions could be planted in mass upsurges for just responses to climate change or in other mass struggles.[16]

There are many possible futures. It is impossible to predict if or how such a revolutionary breakthrough will happen. A breakthrough anywhere would be world-historic, and would reverberate globally, encouraging people elsewhere to repeat its success. There can be no doubt that capitalism will cause profound societal crises in the years ahead. These are likely to create situations in which both bloody repression and social revolution are possible outcomes. The case for ecosocialism does not depend on a rosy view of what lies ahead. Even if it turns out that capitalism does so much damage to the Earth System that ecological apocalypse becomes eventually inevitable, it will still make sense to fight for ecosocialism as palliative care for humanity.[17] Let us give the last word to the 2014 Lima Ecosocialist Declaration:

> If there is any escape from climate change and the global ecological crisis, it will emerge from the power of struggle and the organization of the oppressed and exploited peoples of the world, with the understanding that the struggle for a world without ecological destruction must connect to the struggle for a society without oppression or exploitation. This change must begin now, bringing together unique struggles, daily efforts, processes of self-management, and reforms to slow the crisis, with a vision centred on a change of civilization, a new society in harmony with nature.[18]

Some Suggestions for Further Reading

On the ecological crisis, capitalism, and the need for eco-socialism, Ian Angus, *Facing the Anthropocene: Fossil Capitalism and the Crisis of the Earth System* (New York: Monthly Review Press, 2016) is an excellent introduction.

I have tried to provide an accessible introduction to the theoretical perspective I think can best understand society and inform struggles for transformation in *We Can Do Better: Ideas for Changing Society* (Winnipeg: Fernwood, 2017). To better understand capitalism in particular, I suggest starting with David McNally, *Global Slump: The Economics and Politics of Crisis and Resistance* (Oakland: PM Press, 2011) and Hadas Thier, *A People's Guide to Capitalism: An Introduction to Marxist Economics* (Chicago: Haymarket Books, 2020). On capital as fossil capital, see chapter thirteen of Andreas Malm's *Fossil Capital: The Rise of Steam Power and the Roots of Global Warming* (London: Verso, 2016).

Although this book has argued against part of what Malm argues in *How to Blow Up a Pipeline: Learning to Fight in a World on Fire* (London: Verso, 2021), Malm's book is worth reading for its eloquent arguments against pacifism and despair and for the need to escalate the struggle for climate justice reforms. Jonathan Neale's *Fight the Fire: Green New Deals and Global Climate Jobs* (London: Resistance Books, 2021) provides a clear and comprehensive look at the range of changes that need to be made as part of a just transition.

Harsha Walia's *Border and Rule: Global Migration, Capitalism, and the Rise of Racist Nationalism* (Chicago: Haymarket Books, 2021) analyzes important forces in the world today that climate justice supporters must understand.

The online journal *Climate & Capitalism*, edited by Ian Angus, is a valuable resource, including for its reading lists. https://climateandcapitalism.com.

Notes

Foreword

1   CBC News: The National, "Lytton, B.C., Evacuated after Wildfire Engulfs Community," July 1, 2021, https://www.youtube.com/watch?v=Ft5hOrN_uVM.

2   Cathy Kearney, "B.C. Man Says He Watched in Horror as Lytton Wildfire Claimed the Lives of His Parents," CBC News, July 2, 2021, https://www.cbc.ca/news/canada/british-columbia/son-recounts-horror-of-losing-parents-in-lytton-bc-fire-1.6088297.

3   Fred Pearce, "Global Extinction Rates: Why Do Estimates Vary So Wildly?," *Yale Environment 360*, August 17, 2015, https://e360.yale.edu/features/global_extinction_rates_why_do_estimates_vary_so_wildly.

4   Dharna Noor, "Poor Countries Are Hit Worst by Extreme Weather, but No One Is Safe," Gizmodo, December 4, 2019, https://gizmodo.com/poor-countries-are-hit-worst-by-extreme-weather-but-no-1840183259.

5   "Updating Our Ads and Monetization Policies on Climate Change," Google, October 7, 2021, https://support.google.com/google-ads/answer/11221321?hl=en.

6   "Sustainability at Meta," Meta, accessed January 12, 2022, https://sustainability.fb.com.

7   "The Climate Pledge," Amazon, accessed January 12, 2022, https://sustainability.aboutamazon.com/about/the-climate-pledge.

8   Dharna Noor, "Big Oil's Climate Plans Fail at Every Metric," Gizmodo, September 23, 2020, https://gizmodo.com/big-oil-s-climate-plans-fail-at-every-metric-1845146708.

9   Brian Merchant, "How Google, Microsoft, and Big Tech Are Automating the Climate Crisis," Gizmodo, February 21, 2019, https://gizmodo.com/how-google-microsoft-and-big-tech-are-automating-the-1832790799.

10 "UNDP: More Spent on Fossil Fuel Subsidies Than Fighting Poverty," Africa Renewal, October 29, 2021, https://www.un.org/africarenewal/magazine/november-2021/undp-more-spent-fossil-fuel-subsidies-fighting-poverty.

11   Dharna Noor, "Extreme Heat Could Cause as Many Deaths as All Infectious Diseases Combined," Gizmodo, August 4, 2020, https://gizmodo.com/extreme-heat-could-cause-as-many-deaths-as-all-infectio-1844608336.

12   Dharna Noor, "This Hauntingly Beautiful Image Shows Greenland's Massive Melt," Gizmodo, August 24, 2021, https://gizmodo.com/this-hauntingly-beautiful-image-shows-greenland-s-massi-1847546651.

13   Dharna Noor, "The Climate Crisis May Have Helped Spawn Massive Locust Swarms in East Africa," Gizmodo, January 31, 2020, https://gizmodo.com/the-climate-crisis-may-have-helped-spawn-massive-locust-1841385871.

14   Josie Garthwaite, "Climate Change Has Worsened Global Economic Inequality," Stanford University, April 22, 2019, https://earth.stanford.edu/news/climate-change-has-worsened-global-economic-inequality#gs.m6k58y.

1.   The Path We're On

1   "Global Warming of 1.5°C." Intergovernmental Panel on Climate Change, 2018, https://www.ipcc.ch/sr15.

2   "Temperatures," Climate Action Tracker, February 2022, https://climateactiontracker.org/global/temperatures. The projections of climate science models are, of course, evolving.

3   Andreas Malm, *Fossil Capital: The Rise of Steam Power and the Roots of Global Warming* (London: Verso, 2016), 383.

4   David Wallace-Wells, *The Uninhabitable Earth* (New York: Tim Duggan Books, 2019), 11. For a summary of the IPCC's latest report on the science of climate change, see "In-depth Q&A: The IPCC's Sixth Assessment Report on Climate Change," Carbon Brief, August 9, 2021, https://www.carbonbrief.org/in-depth-qa-the-ipccs-sixth-assessment-report-on-climate-science. For a brief comment on how this report "obscures the systemic roots of climate change," see Steve D'Arcy, "Ideology and the New IPCC Report," August 9, 2021, *Public Autonomy* blog, https://publicautonomy.org/2021/08/09/ipcc.

5   Hubertus Fischer et al., "Paleoclimate Constraints on the Impact of 2° Anthropogenic Warming and Beyond," *Nature Geoscience* 11 (2018): 474–85; Will Steffen et al., "Trajectories of the Earth System in the Anthropocene," *Proceedings of the National Academy of Sciences* 115, no. 33 (2018): 8252–59.

6   Richard Seymour, "Lights Out for the Species," November 4, 2018, https://www.patreon.com/posts/lights-out-for-22503914.

7   Will Steffen et al., "Planetary Boundaries; Guiding Human Development on a Changing Planet," *Science* 347, no. 6223 (February 2015): 736–47, http://doi.org/10.1126/science.1259855.

8   Ian Angus, *Facing the Anthropocene: Fossil Capitalism and the Crisis of the Earth System* (New York: Monthly Review Press, 2016).

9   Eddie Yuen, "The Politics of Failure Have Failed: The Environmental Movement and Catastrophism," in Sasha Lilley, David McNally, Eddie Yuen, and James Davis, *Catastrophism: The Apocalyptic Politics of Collapse and Rebirth* (Oakland: PM Press, 2012), 130.

10 Camilo Mora et al., "Broad Threat to Humanity from Cumulative Climate Hazards Intensified by Greenhouse Gas Emissions," *Nature Climate Change* 8 (November 2018): 1062, 1068.

11 Wallace-Wells, *The Uninhabitable Earth*, 40–41.

12 Ashley Dawson, *Extreme Cities: The Peril and Promise of Urban Life in the Age of Climate Change* (London: Verso, 2017), 30.

13 Dawson, *Extreme Cities*, 62.

14 I use "neoliberal" to describe the way of organizing capitalism that gradually emerged and spread beginning in the late 1970s, after the long economic boom that followed the Second World War had come to an end. See David McNally, *Global Slump: The Economics and Politics of Crisis and Resistance* (Oakland: PM Press, 2011), 25–60.

15 Tania López-Marrero and Ben Wisner, "Not in the Same Boat: Disasters and Differential Vulnerability in the Insular Caribbean," *Caribbean Studies* 40, no. 2 (2012): 129–68. This is not to deny that Cuba is a bureaucratic dictatorship—see Samuel Farber, *Cuba Since the Revolution of 1959: A Critical Assessment* (Chicago: Haymarket Books, 2011).

16 Joel Wainwright and Geoff Mann, *Climate Leviathan: A Political Theory of Our Planetary Future* (London: Verso, 2018), 132–33.

17 Dawson, *Extreme Cities*, 219.

18 Wainwright and Mann, *Climate Leviathan*, 133.

19 Malm, *Fossil Capital*, 391.

20 "Why Eko Atlantic?" Eko Atlantic, accessed February 3, 2021, http://www.ekoatlantic.com/why-eko-atlantic.

21 Martin Lukacs, "New, Privatized African City Heralds Climate Apartheid," *Guardian*, January 21, 2014, https://www.theguardian.com/environment/true-north/2014/jan/21/new-privatized-african-city-heralds-climate-apartheid.

22 Simon Pirani, *Burning Up: A Global History of Fossil Fuel Consumption* (London: Pluto Press, 2018), 2.

23 For data on emissions, see "CO_2 and Greenhouse Gas Emissions," Our World in Data, updated August 2020, http://ourworldindata.org/co2-and-other-greenhouse-gas-emissions.

24 Pirani, *Burning Up*, 173.

25 Pirani, 47–50.

26 Pirani, 179.

27 Gareth Dale, "Economic Growth: A Short History," *Ecologist*, June 18, 2019, https://theecologist.org/2019/jun/18/economic-growth-short-history.

28 Cinzia Arruzza, Tithi Bhattacharya, and Nancy Fraser, *Feminism for the 99%: A Manifesto* (London: Verso, 2019), 64.

29   For a brief introduction to capitalism, see David Camfield, *We Can Do Better: Ideas for Changing Society* (Winnipeg: Fernwood Publishing, 2017), 55–67. For more, see McNally, *Global Slump*.

30   Malm, *Fossil Capital*, 267–68.

31   Angus, *Facing the Anthropocene*, 171. For analysis of why capital became fossil capital, see Malm, *Fossil Capital*, 279–326.

32   Angus, *Facing the Anthropocene*, 113–22.

33   David Ciplet, J. Timmons Roberts, and Mizan R. Khan, *Power in a Warming World: The New Global Politics of Climate Change and the Remaking of Environmental Inequality* (Cambridge, MA: MIT Press, 2015), 152.

34   Éric Pineault, "The Capitalist Pressure to Extract: The Ecological and Political Economy of Extreme Oil in Canada," *Studies in Political Economy* 99, no. 2 (2018): 138, 141.

35   Naomi Klein, *This Changes Everything: Capitalism vs. the Climate* (Toronto: Alfred A. Knopf Canada, 2014).

36   Max Roser and Hannah Ritchie, "Hunger and Undernourishment," Our World in Data, accessed February 3, 2021, http://ourworldindata.org/hunger-and-undernourishment.

37   Camfield, *We Can Do Better*, 70–75.

38   Michael Roberts, *The Long Depression: How It Happened, Why It Happened, and What Happens Next* (Chicago: Haymarket Books, 2016), 114.

39   Richard Seymour, *Against Austerity: How We Can Fix the Crisis They Made* (London: Pluto Press, 2014), 3.

40   Lorna Finlayson, "Travelling in the Wrong Direction," *London Review of Books* 41, no. 13, (July 4, 2019): 7.

41   Robert Chernomas, Ian Hudson, and Mark Hudson, *Neoliberal Lives: Work, Politics, and Health in the Contemporary United States* (Manchester: Manchester University Press, 2019); Danny Dorling, "Austerity Bites—Falling Life Expectancy in the UK," *BMJ Opinion*, March 19, 2019, https://blogs.bmj.com/bmj/2019/03/19/danny-dorling.

42   Rob Wallace, Alex Liebman, Luis Fernando Chaves, and Rodrick Wallace, "COVID-19 and Circuits of Capital," *Monthly Review* 72, no. 1 (May 2020): 1–15, https://monthlyreview.org/2020/05/01/covid-19-and-circuits-of-capital. On capitalism and pandemics, see also Andreas Malm, *Corona, Climate, Chronic Emergency: War Communism in the Twenty-First Century* (London: Verso, 2020).

43   This term has been used to refer to quite different things. See "Just Transition—Just What is It? An Analysis of Language, Strategies and Projects," Labor Network for Sustainability, accessed February 4, 2021, https://www.labor4sustainability.org/uncategorized/just-transition-just-what-is-it.

44   Intergovernmental Panel on Climate Change, *Global Warming of 1.5°C.* (2018), 15, https://www.ipcc.ch/sr15. Because the IPCC's models assume the large-scale use of methods to remove CO_2 from the

atmosphere (negative emissions), methods that are unproven at that scale and whose possible future deployment can be used today to justify delaying cutting emissions, some climate scientists argue that emissions need to be cut more quickly. For example, see Neil Grant and Ajay Gambhir, "Guest Post: Emissions Should Fall 'Twice as Fast' in Case Negative Emissions Fail," Carbon Brief, June 28, 2021, https:// www.carbonbrief.org/guest-post-emissions-should-fall-twice-as-fast-in-case-negative-emissions-fail.

45 James Dyke, Robert Watson, and Wolfgang Knorr, "Climate Scientists: Concept of Net Zero Is a Dangerous Trap," *The Conversation*, April 22, 2021, https://theconversation.com/climate-scientists-concept-of-net-zero-is-a-dangerous-trap-157368.

46 Stan Cox, *The Green New Deal and Beyond: Ending the Climate Emergency While We Still Can* (San Francisco: City Lights, 2020), 81.

47 For a scientific model of how emissions and energy use could be reduced in a just way, see Arnulf Grubler et al., "A Low Energy Demand Scenario for Meeting the 1.5° C Target and Sustainable Development Goals without Negative Emissions Technologies," *Nature Energy* 3, no. 6 (2018): 515–27, https://doi.org/10.1038/s41560-018-0172-6.

48 Mathew Abbott and Steven Chang, "The Victorian 'Green New Deal' Is Really an Exercise in Greenwashing," *Jacobin*, February 4, 2021, https:// jacobinmag.com/2021/02/victoria-australia-daniel-andrews-labor-greenwashing-green-new-deal. On different kinds of GND, see Natasha Heenan and Anna Sturman, "Five Orientations to the Green New Deal," Progress in Political Economy, March 30, 2020, https://www.ppesydney. net/5-orientations-to-the-green-new-deal/ and Max Ajl, *A People's Green New Deal* (London: Pluto Press, 2021), 75–95.

49 Kate Aronoff, Alyssa Battistoni, Daniel Aldana Cohen, and Thea Riofrancos, *A Planet to Win: Why We Need a Green New Deal* (London: Verso, 2019), 16–19. The Sanders GND aims to cut US GHG emissions by at least 71 percent by 2030 and also reduce emissions from countries in the Global South by half that amount on the same timescale. On why a GND in a rich country like the US should eliminate fossil fuel use and reduce energy demand, see Cox, *Green New Deal*, 51–82.

50 See, for example, www.ecoequity.org and Ajl, *A People's Green New Deal*.

51 While *A People's Green New Deal* makes valid criticisms of various GNDs, Ajl's alternative "is about building eco-socialism" (115) as he understands it (which differs from the understanding briefly sketched at the end of this book). My approach is different: instead of laying out a broad range of radical reforms intended to get rid of capitalism, the aim of this book is to analyze what it would take to achieve a minimum emergency program for a just transition. It says very little about the contents of such a program, focusing instead on what has received much too little serious attention: what would it take to actually achieve that? Winning a just transition in my sense of the term would be an

extraordinary accomplishment, and the process of doing so would also create possibilities for deeper change. On Ajl's book, see David Camfield, "Building Eco-Socialism: A Review of Max Ajl's *A People's Green New Deal*," *Tempest*, July 22, 2021, https://www.tempestmag.org/2021/07/building-eco-socialism.

52 Dina Gilio-Whitaker, *As Long as the Grass Grows: The Indigenous Fight for Environmental Justice, from Colonization to Standing Rock* (Boston: Beacon Press, 2019), 36. As Gilio-Whitaker notes (50–51), settler colonialism has a logic of eliminating Indigenous people as such. This is what makes it genocidal. Genocide does not necessarily mean intentionally attempting to kill a population in the way the Nazis set out to do to Jews in Europe.

2. Will Capitalists Save Us? What about Governments?

1   Joel Solomon, "Regarding Pigs: A Note on the Cover of this Edition," in Joel Solomon with Tyee Bridge, *The Clean Money Revolution: Reinventing Power, Purpose and Capitalism* (Gabriola Island, BC: New Society Publishers, 2017), v.

2   Solomon with Bridge, *Clean Money*, 161.

3   Solomon with Bridge, 185.

4   L. Hunter Lovins and Boyd Cohen, *Climate Capitalism: Capitalism in the Age of Climate Change* (New York: Hill and Wang, 2011), 27.

5   Gavin Fridell and Martijn Konings, "Introduction: Neoliberal Capitalism as the Age of Icons," in Fridell and Konings, eds., *Age of Icons: Exploring Philanthrocapitalism in the Contemporary World* (Toronto: University of Toronto Press, 2013), 17.

6   On such claims about positive thinking, see Barbara Ehrenreich, *Bright-Sided: How Positive Thinking Is Undermining America* (New York: Picador, 2009).

7   These emissions are estimated to have fallen to 34 gigatonnes in 2020 because of the impact of the COVID-19 pandemic. "Global Carbon Project: Coronavirus Causes 'Record Fall' in Fossil-Fuel Emissions in 2020," *Carbon Brief*, December 11, 2020, https://www.carbonbrief.org/global-carbon-project-coronavirus-causes-record-fall-in-fossil-fuel-emissions-in-2020.

8   David McNally, *Global Slump: The Economics and Politics of Crisis and Resistance* (Oakland: PM Press, 2011), 76.

9   Tariq Ali, *The Extreme Centre: A Second Warning* (London: Verso, 2018).

10 Although some of these parties are readily adapting to policies that give governments a different role in reviving capital's profits than the role assigned by neoliberal ideology, policies which are designed to respond to the long depression and the recession triggered by the COVID-19 pandemic in particular, they remain deeply influenced by neoliberal ideology.

11 Rainforest Action Network, *Tipping the Scales: 100 Days to Secure a Real Climate Legacy* (San Francisco: Rainforest Action Network, 2016), 2, https://www.ran.org/wp-content/uploads/2018/06/RAN_Tipping_the_Scales_vFINAL_(1).pdf.

12 Lance Selfa, "From Hope to Despair: How the Obama Years Gave Us Trump," in Lance Selfa, ed., *US Politics in an Age of Uncertainty: Essays on a New Reality* (Chicago: Haymarket Books, 2017), 111–24.

13 Keeanga-Yamahtta Taylor, "Black Politics in the Trump Era," in Selfa, *US Politics in an Age of Uncertainty*, 129.

14 For analysis of Biden's initial policies, see Ashley Smith, "Imperialist Keynesianism: Biden's Program for Rehabilitating US Capitalism," *Tempest*, May 18, 2021, https://www.tempestmag.org/2021/05/imperialist-keynesianism.

15 Martin Lukacs, *The Trudeau Formula: Seduction and Betrayal in an Age of Discontent* (Montreal: Black Rose Books, 2019), 124.

16 Lukacs, *The Trudeau Formula*, 102.

17 "Canada Country Summary," Climate Action Tracker, updated September 21, 2020, http://climateactiontracker.org/countries/canada.

18 Lukacs, *The Trudeau Formula*, 185.

19 Lukacs, 138.

20 Bill Curry and Kate McCullough, "Trudeau Changes Tone, Says Rail Barricades 'Must Come Down Now," *Globe and Mail*, February 21, 2020, https://www.theglobeandmail.com/canada/article-barricades-at-rail-crossings-must-now-come-down-trudeau-says.

21 Lorène Lavocat, "Le bilan de Hollande sur l'écologie: trés décevant," *Reporterre*, May 13, 2017, https://reporterre.net/Le-bilan-de-Hollande-sur-l-ecologie-tres-decevant.

22 Stefan Kipfer, "Projecting Shadows: France Before the 2017 Elections," *The Bullet*, March 5, 2017, https://socialistproject.ca/2017/03/b1378.

23 Gerard De Trolio, "The NDP's Oil Problem," *Jacobin*, April 27, 2018, https://jacobinmag.com/2018/04/the-ndps-oil-problem.

24 For example, see Joachim Jachnow, "What's Become of the German Greens?," *New Left Review* 81 (May–June 2013): 95–117, https://newleftreview.org/issues/II81/articles/joachim-jachnow-what-s-become-of-the-german-greens.

25 Panagiotis Sotiris, "Disciplined and Punished," *Jacobin*, August 31, 2018, https://www.jacobinmag.com/2018/08/greece-syriza-tsipras-memoranda-austerity-odyssey.

26 Sotiris, "Disciplined and Punished."

27 Ciplet, Roberts, and Khan, *Power*, 152.

28 Camfield, *We Can Do Better*, 63–64; Simon Clarke, "State, Class Struggle, and the Reproduction of Capital," *Kapitalistate* no. 10/11 (1983): 113–34.

3.   Mass Movements: Our Only Hope

1   David Roediger, *Seizing Freedom: Slave Emancipation and Liberty for All* (London: Verso, 2014), 17, 38, 5.

2   Brian Kelly, "Slave Self-Activity and the Bourgeois Revolution in the United States: Jubilee and the Boundaries of Black Freedom," *Historical Materialism* 27, no. 3 (2019): 31–76.

3   Robin Blackburn, *The American Crucible: Slavery, Emancipation and Human Rights* (London: Verso, 2011), 392.

4   "Bernie Sanders Defines His Vision for Democratic Socialism in the United States," *Vox*, June 12, 2019, https://www.vox.com/2019/6/12/18663217/bernie-sanders-democratic-socialism-speech-transcript.

5   "Bernie Sanders Defines His Vision."

6   Howard Zinn, *A People's History of the United States* (New York: Perennial Classics, 2003), 392, 293.

7   Charles Post, "The New Deal and the Popular Front: Models for Contemporary Socialists?," *International Socialist Review* 108 (March 2018), https://isreview.org/issue/108/new-deal-and-popular-front.

8   David Zachariah and Petter Nilsson, "Waiting in the Wings," *Jacobin*, March 15, 2016, https://www.jacobinmag.com/2016/03/sweden-socialism-welfare-state-trade-union.

9   Ian Birchall, *Bailing Out the System: Reformist Socialism in Western Europe 1944–1985* (London: Bookmarks, 1986), 49.

10   Leon Trotsky, *The History of the Russian Revolution* (New York: Pathfinder, 1980), xvii.

11   Jonathan Matthew Smucker, *Hegemony How-To: A Roadmap for Radicals* (Chico, CA: AK Press, 2017), chapter six contains some useful thoughts about organizing in the US context. However, Smucker's strategy for changing society is quite different from the one argued for in this book.

12   Tobi Haslett, "Magic Actions: Looking Back on the George Floyd Rebellion," *N+1*, May 7, 2021, https://nplusonemag.com/online-only/online-only/magic-actions/.

13   Larry Buchanan, Quoctrung Bui, and Jugal K. Patel, "Black Lives Matter May Be the Largest Movement in US History," *New York Times*, July 3, 2020, https://www.nytimes.com/interactive/2020/07/03/us/george-floyd-protests-crowd-size.html.

14   Rushdia Mehreen and David Gray-Donald, "Spring 2015 Anti-austerity Movement in Québec: A Critical Retrospective of the Organizing," *Canadian Dimension*, October 21, 2015, https://canadiandimension.com/articles/view/spring-2015-anti-austerity-movement-in-quebec-a-critical-perspective.

15   Ben Beckett, "Sickouts and Strike Threats Stopped the Government Shutdown," *Jacobin*, January 25, 2019, https://jacobinmag.com/2019/01/government-shutdown-collective-action-strikes-unions.

16 "Four Principles of the Red Deal," *The Red Nation*, June 25, 2019, https://
therednation.org/2019/06/25/four-principles-of-the-red-deal.

17 Simon Hannah, "Corbynism—Where Has the Mass Movement Gone?"
Open Democracy, January 25, 2019, https://www.opendemocracy.net/en/
opendemocracyuk/corbynism-has-wasted-opportunity-to-transform-
labour-and-democracy.

18 Varshini Prakash, "Organize. Vote. Strike.," in Varshini Prakash and
Guido Girgenti, eds., *Winning the Green New Deal: Why We Must, How
We Can* (New York: Simon and Schuster, 2020), 279.

19 Alain Bertho, *The Age of Violence: The Crisis of Political Action and the
End of Utopia*, trans. David Broder (London: Verso, 2018), 31.

20 Thomas Nicholas, Galen Hall, and Colleen Schmidt, "The Faulty Science,
Doomism and Flawed Conclusions of Deep Adaptation," *Open Democracy*,
July 14, 2020, https://www.opendemocracy.net/en/oureconomy/
faulty-science-doomism-and-flawed-conclusions-deep-adaptation.

21 Gabriel Levy, "Disaster Environmentalism 1: Looking the Future in the
Face," *People and Nature* blog, December 5, 2019, https://peopleandnature.
wordpress.com/2019/12/05/disaster-evironmentalism-1-looking-the-
future-in-the-face.

22 Paul Kingsnorth, "Life versus the Machine," *Orion* 37, no. 4 (Winter 2018),
https://orionmagazine.org/article/life-versus-the-machine. Kingsnorth
cowrote the Dark Mountain Project's manifesto, which claims that, far
from capitalism being the problem, "the roots" of "the converging crises
of our times . . . lie in the stories we have been telling ourselves" (Paul
Kingsnorth and Dougald Hine, "Uncivilisation," Dark Mountain Project,
2009, http://dark-mountain.net/about/manifesto). This is naked ideal-
ism, on which see Camfield, *We Can Do Better*, 6–11.

23 Paul Kingsnorth, "The Lie of the Land: Does Environmentalism Have
a Future in the Age of Trump?," *Guardian*, March 18, 2017, https://
www.theguardian.com/books/2017/mar/18/the-new-lie-of-the-
land-what-future-for-environmentalism-in-the-age-of-trump. For a
critique, see "Lies of the Land: Against and Beyond Paul Kingsnorth's
Völkish Environmentalism," *Out of the Woods*, March 31, 2017, http://
libcom.org/blog/lies-land-against-beyond-paul-kingsnorth's-völkisch-
environmentalism-31032017.

24 Stephen D'Arcy, *Languages of the Unheard: Why Militant Protest Is Good
for Democracy* (Toronto: Between the Lines, 2013), 185.

25 D'Arcy, *Languages of the Unheard*, 185–86.

26 Naomi Klein, "Let Them Drown: The Violence of Othering in a Warming
World," *London Review of Books* 38, no. 11 (June 2, 2016), https://www.
lrb.co.uk/v38/n11/naomi-klein/let-them-drown.

27 For some analysis of why this is the case, see Camfield, *We Can Do Better*,
100–108.

28 See various XR websites and Roger Hallam, "The Civil Resistance Model," in Clare Farrell et al., eds., *This Is Not a Drill: An Extinction Rebellion Handbook* (London: Penguin Books, 2019), 99–105.

29 Pip Henman, "What Kind of Rebellion Will It Take to Save Humanity from Extinction?," *Climate and Capitalism*, August 6, 2019, https://climateandcapitalism.com/2019/08/06/what-kind-of-rebellion-will-save-humanity-from-extinction.

30 *Salvage* editorial board, "Extinction Rebellion," April 26, 2019, https://www.patreon.com/posts/salvage-monthly-26373652.

31 Nafeez Ahmed, "The Flawed Social Science Behind Extinction Rebellion's Change Strategy," *Medium*, October 28, 2019, https://medium.com/insurge-intelligence/the-flawed-science-behind-extinction-rebellions-change-strategy-af077b9abb4d (emphasis removed).

32 Andreas Malm, *How to Blow Up a Pipeline: Learning to Fight in a World on Fire* (London: Verso, 2021), 61.

33 Élodie Chédikian, Paul Guillibert, and Davide Gallo Lassere, "The Climate of Roundabouts: The *Gilets Jaunes* and Environmentalism," *South Atlantic Quarterly* 119, no. 4 (2020): 879. See also Stathis Kouvelakis, "The French Insurgency: Political Economy of the Gilets Jaunes," *New Left Review* no. 116/117 (March–June 2019): 75–98.

34 Keeanga-Yamahtta Taylor, "Think the Women's March Wasn't Radical Enough? Do Something About It!," *Guardian*, January 24, 2017, https://www.theguardian.com/commentisfree/2017/jan/24/women-march-diversity-minorities-working-class.

35 Keith Brower Brown, Jeremy Gong, Matt Huber, and Jamie Munro, "A Real Green New Deal Means Class Struggle," *Jacobin*, March 21, 2019, https://jacobinmag.com/2019/03/green-new-deal-class-struggle-organizing.

36 See Tara Olivetree (Ehrcke), "Power, Workers and the Fight for Climate Justice," *Midnight Sun*, July 12, 2021, https://www.midnightsunmag.ca/power-workers-and-the-fight-for-climate-justice/. Kim Moody's books *In Solidarity: Essays on Working-Class Organization in the United States* (Chicago: Haymarket Books, 2014) and *On New Terrain: How Capital Is Reshaping the Battleground of Class War* (Chicago: Haymarket Books, 2017) are important, and not just for readers in the US. On Canadian unions, see my *Canadian Labour in Crisis: Reinventing the Workers' Movement* (Winnipeg: Fernwood Publishing, 2011). The international network Trade Unions for Energy Democracy is an important resource for union activists who support climate justice. On how some Quebec workers struck as part of the global climate strike of September 2019, see Alain Savard, "How Seven Thousand Quebec Workers Went on Strike against Climate Change," *Labor Notes*, October 25, 2019, https://labornotes.org/2019/10/how-seven-thousand-quebec-workers-went-strike-against-climate-change.

37 Andreas Malm, *How to Blow Up a Pipeline*, 69.

38 Malm, *How to Blow Up a Pipeline*, 50.

39 Leon Trotsky, "The Marxist Position on Individual Terrorism," in Trotsky, *Against Individual Terrorism* (New York: Pathfinder, 1974), 7.

40 Acts of sabotage carried out openly by large numbers of people are a form of mass direct action, and a different tactic than what Malm argues for.

41 Nancy Fraser, "Climates of Capital: For a Trans-Environmental Eco-Socialism," *New Left Review* no. 127 (January–February 2021): 122.

4. "Even a Ravaged Planet Is Worth Fighting For"

1 The phrase that forms the title of this chapter is taken from "Salvage Perspectives #1: Amid this Stony Rubbish," *Salvage* no. 1, August 10, 2015, http://salvage.zone/in-print/salvage-perspectives-1-amid-this-stony-rubbish.

2 Alan Silverman, "Can the Climate Justice Movement Succeed?," *Monitor* 27, no. 5 (January–February 2021): 34, https://www.policyalternatives.ca/sites/default/files/uploads/publications/National%20Office/2020/12/CCPA%20Monitor%20Jan%20Feb%202021%20WEB.pdf.

3 There are many problems with nuclear power, including the GHGs emitted through the full course of the processes involved, the amount of water used, the need to store radioactive waste, the harm done to Indigenous peoples by uranium mining, the diversion of money that could be spent expanding renewable energy generation instead, and the risk of damage to reactors (for example, by extreme weather) leading to the release of radiation. For a collection of articles on the topic including pieces by supporters of nuclear power, see https://climateandcapitalism.com/category/nuclear.

4 Joel Wainwright and Geoff Mann, *Climate Leviathan: A Political Theory of Our Planetary Future* (London: Verso, 2018), 149. There are serious reasons to doubt the ability of competing capitalist states to actually set up and maintain such an institution, but that does not rule out the possibility that some states may attempt to create SRM schemes.

5 Richard Seymour, "Minimalist Democracy: The Antipolitics of the Right," August 14, 2019, https://www.patreon.com/posts/minimalist-of-29092839.

6 Geoff Mann and Joel Wainwright, "Political Scenarios for Climate Disaster," *Dissent* 66, no. 3 (Summer 2019): 65–72, https://www.dissentmagazine.org/article/political-scenarios-for-climate-disaster.

7 Dan Boscov-Ellen, "Infectious Optimism: Notes on COVID-19 and Climate Change," *Spectre*, May 27, 2020, https://spectrejournal.com/infectious-optimism.

8 Andreas Malm, *How to Blow Up a Pipeline: Learning to Fight in a World on Fire* (London: Verso, 2021), 146, 147.

9 Naomi Klein, "Let Them Drown: The Violence of Othering in a Warming World," *London Review of Books* 38, no. 11 (June 2, 2016), https://www.lrb.co.uk/v38/n11/naomi-klein/let-them-drown

10   Jonathan Neale, "Social Collapse and Climate Breakdown," *Ecologist*, May 8, 2019, https://theecologist.org/2019/may/08/social-collapse-and-climate-breakdown.

11   Andreas Malm, "Revolution in a Warming World: Lessons from the Russian to the Syrian Revolutions," *The Bullet*, April 23, 2018, https://socialistproject.ca/2018/04/revolution-in-a-warming-world/.

12   Out of the Woods Collective, *Hope against Hope: Writings on Ecological Crisis* (Brooklyn: Common Notions, 2020), 231.

13   Rebecca Solnit, *A Paradise Built in Hell: The Extraordinary Communities That Arise in Disaster* (New York: Viking, 2009), 8.

14   Michael Löwy, "The Paris Commune: A Tiger's Leap into the Past," *Midnight Sun*, May 26, 2021, https://www.midnightsunmag.ca/the-paris-commune-a-tigers-leap-into-the-past.

15   Neale, "Social Collapse."

16   Nick Serpe, "Indigenous Resistance Is Post-Apocalyptic, with Nick Estes," *Dissent*, July 31, 2019, https://www.dissentmagazine.org/online_articles/booked-indigenous-resistance-is-post-apocalyptic-with-nick-estes.

17   Jeff Noonan, *Materialist Ethics and Life-Value* (Montreal and Kingston: McGill-Queen's University Press, 2012), 23.

18   Thea Riofrancos, "Plan, Mood, Battlefield—Reflections on the Green New Deal," *Viewpoint Magazine*, May 16, 2019, https://www.viewpointmag.com/2019/05/16/plan-mood-battlefield-reflections-on-the-green-new-deal/.

19   Rosie Warren, "Some Final Words on Pessimism," *Salvage* no. 2 (November 2015): 105.

20   Terry Eagleton, *Hope without Optimism* (Charlottesville: University of Virginia Press, 2015), 48, 43.

21   Sai Englert, "Settlers, Workers, and the Logic of Accumulation by Dispossession," *Antipode* 52, no. 6 (2020): 1647–66.

22   Serpe, "Indigenous Resistance."

23   Nick Estes, *Our History Is the Future: Standing Rock versus the Dakota Access Pipeline, and the Long Tradition of Indigenous Resistance* (London: Verso, 2019).

24   Andreas Malm, "The Walls of the Tank: On Palestinian Resistance," *Salvage* no. 4 (February 2017): 21, 32, 26, 40, 44, 52.

25   Alex De Jong, "Being Brave Because It Is Right," *Jacobin*, April 13, 2017, https://www.jacobinmag.com/2017/04/henk-sneevliet-marx-lenin-luxemburg-front-indonesia-communists-internationalism.

26   Nathaniel Flakin, *Martin Monath: A Jewish Resistance Fighter Among Nazi Soldiers* (London: Pluto Press, 2019); "Trotskyism in Occupied France," Marxists Internet Archive, accessed February 8, 2021, https://www.marxists.org/history/etol/newspape/soldat/broder.htm.

27   Marek Edelman, *The Ghetto Fights* (London: Bookmarks, 1990), 37.

5. Ecosocialism

1   Jean-Francois Bastin et al., "The Global Tree Restoration Potential," *Science* 365, no. 6448 (2019): 76–79, https://doi.org/10.1126/science.aax0848.

2   George Monbiot, "Dare to Declare Capitalism Dead—Before It Takes Us All Down with It," *Guardian*, April 25, 2019, https://www.theguardian.com/commentisfree/2019/apr/25/capitalism-economic-system-survival-earth.

3   Noonan, *Materialist Ethics.*

4   Göran Therborn, "An Age of Progress?," *New Left Review* no. 99 (May–June 2016): 37.

5   John Bellamy Foster, Brett Clark, and Richard York, *The Ecological Rift: Capitalism's War on the Earth* (New York: Monthly Review, 2010), 75.

6   Michael Löwy, *Ecosocialism: A Radical Alternative to Capitalist Catastrophe* (Chicago: Haymarket Books, 2015), 7. Use value refers to the inherent qualities of goods and services, in contrast to the exchange value of commodities, which is measured in markets in terms of money.

7   "Fourth Declaration of the Lacandon Jungle," 1996, Struggle Archive, accessed February 8, 2021, http://struggle.ws/mexico/ezln/jung4.html.

8   Löwy, *Ecosocialism*, 23, 24–25.

9   ISEE & Degrowth Conference 2021, "George Monbiot: Private Sufficiency, Public Luxury," July 17, 2021, https://www.youtube.com/watch?v=KWRRPed4Ds0.

10 "Stalinism and the Future of Socialism (Part I)," April 2021, in *Victor's Children*, podcast, https://soundcloud.com/user-737267994/episode-3-stalinism-and-the-future-of-socialism-part-i; Aufheben, "What Was the USSR? Part IV: Towards a Theory of the Deformation of Value." Libcom.org, accessed February 8, 2021, https://marx.libcom.org/library/what-was-ussr-aufheben-part-4.

11 Leigh Phillips and Michal Rozworski, *The People's Republic of Walmart: How the World's Biggest Corporations Are Laying the Foundations for Socialism* (London: Verso, 2019), 75.

12 Phillips and Rozworski, *The People's Republic of Walmart*, 31, 244.

13 Evgeny Morozov, "Digital Socialism? The Calculation Debate in the Age of Big Data," *New Left Review* no. 116/117 (March–June 2019): 33–67.

14 In countries of the Global South, this includes many peasants, landless people who aren't engaged in wage work, and other people still living land-based ways of life outside capitalist markets.

15 See Camfield, *We Can Do Better*, 126–27, and Charlie Post, "What Strategy for the US Left?," *Jacobin*, February 23, 2018, https://www.jacobinmag.com/2018/02/socialist-organization-strategy-electoral-politics.

16 On how mass struggles can generate new forms of democratic popular power, see Colin Barker, Gareth Dale, and Neil Davidson, eds., *Revolutionary Rehearsals in the Neoliberal Age: Struggling to Be Born?*

(Chicago: Haymarket Books, 2021); Colin Barker, ed., *Revolutionary Rehearsals* (London: Bookmarks, 1987); Samuel Farber, *Before Stalinism: The Rise and Fall of Soviet Democracy* (London: Verso, 1990); Donny Gluckstein, *The Western Soviets: Workers' Councils Versus Parliament 1915–1920* (London: Bookmarks, 1985); and Frank Mintz, *Anarchism and Workers' Self-Management in Revolutionary Spain* (Oakland: AK Press, 2013).

17 The idea of socialism as palliative care is Tara Rose's, quoted in Liza Featherstone, "The Decade When Climate Change Became Real," *Jacobin*, December 31, 2019, https://jacobinmag.com/2019/12/climate-change-decade-standing-rock-greta-thunberg-global-warming.

18 "The Lima Ecosocialist Declaration," in Löwy, *Ecosocialism*, 103.

Index

"Passim" (literally "scattered") indicates intermittent discussion of a topic over a cluster of pages.

About the Authors

David Camfield teaches labour studies and sociology at the University of Manitoba and has been involved in social justice efforts since high school. He is the author of *We Can Do Better: Ideas for Changing Society* and *Canadian Labour in Crisis: Reinventing the Workers' Movement*.

Dharna Noor is a climate and environmental justice journalist who covers climate change for the *Boston Globe*. Previously she worked as a writer for Gizmodo and led the Real News Network's climate team. Her writing has appeared in publications including In These Times, *Jacobin* magazine, and Truthout, and was also featured in a 2021 anthology on climate justice movements called *The World We Need*. She lives in Baltimore.

ABOUT PM PRESS

PM Press is an independent, radical publisher of books and media to educate, entertain, and inspire. Founded in 2007 by a small group of people with decades of publishing, media, and organizing experience, PM Press amplifies the voices of radical authors, artists, and activists. Our aim is to deliver bold political ideas and vital stories to all walks of life and arm the dreamers to demand the impossible. We have sold millions of copies of our books, most often one at a time, face to face. We're old enough to know what we're doing and young enough to know what's at stake. Join us to create a better world.

PM Press
PO Box 23912
Oakland, CA 94623
www.pmpress.org

PM Press in Europe
europe@pmpress.org
www.pmpress.org.uk

FRIENDS OF PM PRESS

These are indisputably momentous times—the financial system is melting down globally and the Empire is stumbling. Now more than ever there is a vital need for radical ideas.

In the many years since its founding—and on a mere shoestring—PM Press has risen to the formidable challenge of publishing and distributing knowledge and entertainment for the struggles ahead. With hundreds of releases to date, we have published an impressive and stimulating array of literature, art, music, politics, and culture. Using every available medium, we've succeeded in connecting those hungry for ideas and information to those putting them into practice.

Friends of PM allows you to directly help impact, amplify, and revitalize the discourse and actions of radical writers, filmmakers, and artists. It provides us with a stable foundation from which we can build upon our early successes and provides a much-needed subsidy for the materials that can't necessarily pay their own way. You can help make that happen—and receive every new title automatically delivered to your door once a month—by joining as a Friend of PM Press. And, we'll throw in a free T-shirt when you sign up.

Here are your options:

- **$30 a month** Get all books and pamphlets plus 50% discount on all webstore purchases

- **$40 a month** Get all PM Press releases (including CDs and DVDs) plus 50% discount on all webstore purchases

- **$100 a month** Superstar—Everything plus PM merchandise, free downloads, and 50% discount on all webstore purchases

For those who can't afford $30 or more a month, we have **Sustainer Rates** at $15, $10 and $5. Sustainers get a free PM Press T-shirt and a 50% discount on all purchases from our website.

Your Visa or Mastercard will be billed once a month, until you tell us to stop. Or until our efforts succeed in bringing the revolution around. Or the financial meltdown of Capital makes plastic redundant. Whichever comes first.

Anthropocene or Capitalocene? Nature, History, and the Crisis of Capitalism

Edited by Jason W. Moore

ISBN: 978-1-62963-148-6
$21.95   304 pages

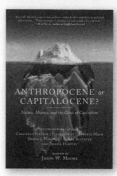

The Earth has reached a tipping point.
Runaway climate change, the sixth great extinction of planetary life, the acidification of the oceans—all point toward an era of unprecedented turbulence in humanity's relationship within the web of life. But just what is that relationship, and how do we make sense of this extraordinary transition?

Anthropocene or Capitalocene? offers answers to these questions from a dynamic group of leading critical scholars. They challenge the theory and history offered by the most significant environmental concept of our times: the Anthropocene. But are we living in the Anthropocene, literally the "Age of Man"? Is a different response more compelling, and better suited to the strange—and often terrifying—times in which we live? The contributors to this book diagnose the problems of Anthropocene thinking and propose an alternative: the global crises of the twenty-first century are rooted in the Capitalocene; not the Age of Man but the Age of Capital.

Anthropocene or Capitalocene? offers a series of provocative essays on nature and power, humanity, and capitalism. Including both well-established voices and younger scholars, the book challenges the conventional practice of dividing historical change and contemporary reality into "Nature" and "Society," demonstrating the possibilities offered by a more nuanced and connective view of human environment-making, joined at every step with and within the biosphere. In distinct registers, the authors frame their discussions within a politics of hope that signal the possibilities for transcending capitalism, broadly understood as a "world-ecology" that joins nature, capital, and power as a historically evolving whole.

Contributors include Jason W. Moore, Eileen Crist, Donna J. Haraway, Justin McBrien, Elmar Altvater, Daniel Hartley, and Christian Parenti.

Global Slump: The Economics and Politics of Crisis and Resistance

David McNally

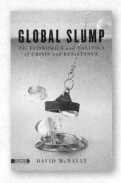

ISBN: 978-1-60486-332-1
$15.95   176 pages

Global Slump analyzes the world financial meltdown as the first systemic crisis of the neoliberal stage of capitalism. It argues that— far from having ended—the crisis has ushered in a whole period of worldwide economic and political turbulence. In developing an account of the crisis as rooted in fundamental features of capitalism, *Global Slump* challenges the view that its source lies in financial deregulation. It offers an original account of the "financialization" of the world economy and explores the connections between international financial markets and new forms of debt and dispossession, particularly in the Global South. The book shows that, while averting a complete meltdown, the massive intervention by central banks laid the basis for recurring crises for poor and working class people. It traces new patterns of social resistance for building an anti-capitalist opposition to the damage that neoliberal capitalism is inflicting on the lives of millions.

"In this book, McNally confirms—once again—his standing as one of the world's leading Marxist scholars of capitalism. For a scholarly, in depth analysis of our current crisis that never loses sight of its political implications (for them and for us), expressed in a language that leaves no reader behind, there is simply no better place to go."
—Bertell Ollman, professor, Department of Politics, NYU, and author of *Dance of the Dialectic: Steps in Marx's Method*

"David McNally's tremendously timely book is packed with significant theoretical and practical insights, and offers actually-existing examples of what is to be done. Global Slump urgently details how changes in the capitalist space-economy over the past 25 years, especially in the forms that money takes, have expanded wide-scale vulnerabilities for all kinds of people, and how people fight back. In a word, the problem isn't neo-liberalism—it's capitalism."
—Ruth Wilson Gilmore, University of Southern California and author, *Golden Gulag: Prisons, Surplus, Crisis, and Opposition in Globalizing California*

Catastrophism: The Apocalyptic Politics of Collapse and Rebirth

Sasha Lilley, David McNally, Eddie Yuen, and James Davis with a foreword by Doug Henwood

ISBN: 978-1-60486-589-9
$16.00   192 pages

We live in catastrophic times. The world is reeling from the deepest economic crisis since the Great Depression, with the threat of further meltdowns ever-looming. Global warming and myriad dire ecological disasters worsen—with little if any action to halt them—their effects rippling across the planet in the shape of almost biblical floods, fires, droughts, and hurricanes. Governments warn that no alternative exists than to take the bitter medicine they prescribe—or risk devastating financial or social collapse. The right, whether religious or secular, views the present as catastrophic and wants to turn the clock back. The left fears for the worst, but hopes some good will emerge from the rubble. Visions of the apocalypse and predictions of impending doom abound. Across the political spectrum, a culture of fear reigns.

Catastrophism explores the politics of apocalypse—on the left and right, in the environmental movement, and from capital and the state—and examines why the lens of catastrophe can distort our understanding of the dynamics at the heart of these numerous disasters—and fatally impede our ability to transform the world. Lilley, McNally, Yuen, and Davis probe the reasons why catastrophic thinking is so prevalent, and challenge the belief that it is only out of the ashes that a better society may be born. The authors argue that those who care about social justice and the environment should eschew the Pandora's box of fear—even as it relates to indisputably apocalyptic climate change. Far from calling people to arms, they suggest, catastrophic fear often results in passivity and paralysis—and, at worst, reactionary politics.

"This groundbreaking book examines a deep current—on both the left and right—of apocalyptical thought and action. The authors explore the origins, uses, and consequences of the idea that collapse might usher in a better world. Catastrophism is a crucial guide to understanding our tumultuous times, while steering us away from the pitfalls of the past."
—Barbara Epstein, author of *Political Protest and Cultural Revolution: Nonviolent Direct Action in the 1970s and 1980s*

The Sea Is Rising and So Are We: A Climate Justice Handbook

Cynthia Kaufman with an Introduction
by Bill McKibben

ISBN: 978-1-62963-865-2
$16.95   192 pages

The Sea is Rising and So Are We: A Climate Justice Handbook is an invitation to get involved in the movement to build a just and sustainable world in the face of the most urgent challenge our species has ever faced. By explaining the entrenched forces that are preventing rapid action, it helps you understand the nature of the political reality we are facing and arms you with the tools you need to overcome them. The book offers background information on the roots of the crisis and the many rapidly expanding solutions that are being implemented all around the world. It explains how to engage in productive messaging that will pull others into the climate justice movement, what you need to know to help build a successful movement, and the policy changes needed to build a world with climate justice. It also explores the personal side, including how engaging in the movement can be good for your mental health. It ends with advice on how you can find the place where you can be the most effective and where you can build climate action into your life in ways that are deeply rewarding.

"The Sea Is Rising and So Are We *is a rare kind of book, at once a primer for activists and an astute commentary on a set of critical topics that even a seasoned climate stalwart could benefit from. It takes on some really tough questions—transformational change, how to talk about the emergency, the need for a specifically global politics of climate justice—and it does in a manner that is both simple and sophisticated. It's not an easy balance, but Kaufman pulls it off."*
—Tom Athanasiou, author of *Dead Heat: Global Justice and Global Warming*

"Cynthia Kaufman's The Sea Is Rising and So Are We *is a valuable overview of where we as a species are in the existential fight to prevent catastrophic climate disruption. It covers a lot, from the UN's Intergovernmental Panel on Climate Change assessment of our situation to the need for a personally supportive movement culture to sustain our climate activism. It is an accessible, up-to-date resource both for those who have been in the climate fight for decades and those who know they need to do so but haven't yet figured out how."*
—Ted Glick, longtime climate organizer and author of *Burglar for Peace*

Against Doom: A Climate Insurgency Manual

Jeremy Brecher

ISBN: 978-1-62963-385-5
$12.95   128 pages

Before the election of Donald Trump the world was already speeding toward climate catastrophe. Now President Trump has jammed his foot on the global warming accelerator. Is there any way for the rest of us to put on the brakes?

Climate insurgency is a strategy for using people power to realize our common interest in protecting the climate. It uses mass, global, nonviolent action to challenge the legitimacy of public and corporate officials who are perpetrating climate destruction.

A global climate insurgency has already begun. It has the potential to halt and roll back Trump's fossil fuel agenda and the global thrust toward climate destruction.

Against Doom: A Climate Insurgency Manual tells how to put that strategy into action—and how it can succeed. It is a handbook for halting global warming and restoring our climate—a how-to for climate insurgents.

"Against Doom *lays out key elements of a far-reaching, global-scaled, pragmatic, people-powered strategy to topple the power of the fossil fuel industry and the institutions behind it.*"
—David Solnit, author of *Globalize Liberation: How to Uproot the System and Build a Better World*

"*In* Against Doom, *Brecher has provided the climate movement with two essential tools: a moral framework for the struggle against fossil fuels, and an actual plan for victory. By blending sober social movement analysis with the fire of grassroots activism, this book shows that there is a genuine, and winnable, case against the fossil fuel economy—a case to be argued in the streets as well as the courtroom. It's an essential volume for anyone committed to social change in the fight against climate change.*"
—Joseph Hamilton, Climate Defense Project

Save the Humans?
Common Preservation in Action

Jeremy Brecher

ISBN: 978-1-62963-798-3
$20.00   272 pages

We the people of the world are creating the conditions for our own self-extermination, whether through the bang of a nuclear holocaust or the whimper of an expiring ecosphere. Today our individual self-preservation depends on common preservation—cooperation to provide for our mutual survival and well-being.

For half a century Jeremy Brecher has been studying and participating in social movements that have created new forms of common preservation. Through entertaining storytelling and personal narrative, *Save the Humans?* provides a unique and revealing interpretation of how social movements arise and how they change the world. Brecher traces a path that leads from the sitdown strikes on the pyramids of ancient Egypt through America's mass strikes and labor revolts to the struggle against economic globalization to today's battles against climate change.

Weaving together personal experience, scholarly research, and historical interpretation, Jeremy Brecher shows how we can construct a "human survival movement" that could "save the humans." He sums up the theme of this book: "I have seen common preservation—and it works." For those seeking an understanding of social movements and an alternative to denial and despair, there is simply no better place to look than *Save the Humans?*

"*This is a remarkable book: part personal story, part intellectual history told in the first person by a skilled writer and assiduous historian, part passionate but clearly and logically argued plea for pushing the potential of collective action to preserve the human race. Easy reading and full of useful and unforgettable stories. . . . A medicine against apathy and political despair much needed in the U.S. and the world today.*"
—Peter Marcuse, author of *Cities for People, Not for Profit: Critical Urban Theory*

Common Preservation: In a Time of Mutual Destruction

Jeremy Brecher
with a Foreword by Todd Vachon

ISBN: 978-1-62963-788-4
$26.95   400 pages

As world leaders eschew cooperation to
address climate change, nuclear proliferation,
economic meltdown, and other threats to
our survival, more and more people experience a pervasive sense of
dread and despair. Is there anything we can do? What can put us on the
course from mutual destruction to common preservation? In the past,
social movements have sometimes made rapid and unexpected changes
that countered apparently incurable social problems. Jeremy Brecher
presents scores of historical examples of people who changed history
by adopting strategies of common preservation, showing what we can
we learn from past social movements to better confront today's global
threats of climate change, war, and economic chaos.

In *Common Preservation*, Brecher shares his experiences and what he has
learned that can help ward off mutual destruction and provides a unique
heuristic—a tool kit for thinkers and activists—to understand and create
new forms of common preservation.

*"Jeremy Brecher's work is astonishing and refreshing; and, God knows,
necessary."*
—Studs Terkel

*"Chapter by chapter, I learn from it; and I admire its ambition. When I
sampled it, it engaged me so much that I set aside other work until I finished
it. Overall, a fine manuscript. Rich in content. Also engaging. Is it not all or
part of a philosophy or worldview?"*
—Charles Lindblom, Sterling Professor Emeritus of Political Science and
Economics at Yale University; author of *The Market System*

*"It is an autobiography of intellectual exploration and of practical
experimentation with the problems of social injustice. It is a project of the
urgent transmission of the lessons learned undertaken under the duress
of historical time which threatens catastrophe. It is a valedictory and an
exhortation."*
—Joshua Dubler, Society of Fellows, Columbia University; author of
Down in the Chapel: Religious Life in an American Prison

Strike!
50th Anniversary Edition

Jeremy Brecher with a Preface by Sara Nelson and a Foreword by Kim Kelly

ISBN: 978-1-62963-800-3
$28.95   640 pages

Jeremy Brecher's *Strike!* narrates the dramatic story of repeated, massive, and sometimes violent revolts by ordinary working people in America. Involving nationwide general strikes, the seizure of vast industrial establishments, nonviolent direct action on a massive scale, and armed battles with artillery and tanks, this exciting hidden history is told from the point of view of the rank-and-file workers who lived it. Encompassing the repeated repression of workers' rebellions by company-sponsored violence, local police, state militias, and the U.S. Army and National Guard, it reveals a dimension of American history rarely found in the usual high school or college history course.

Since its original publication in 1972, no book has done as much as *Strike!* to bring U.S. labor history to a wide audience. Now this fiftieth anniversary edition brings the story up to date with chapters covering the "mini-revolts of the 21st century," including Occupy Wall Street and the Fight for Fifteen. The new edition contains over a hundred pages of new materials and concludes by examining a wide range of current struggles, ranging from #BlackLivesMatter, to the great wave of teachers strikes "for the soul of public education," to the global "Student Strike for Climate," that may be harbingers of mass strikes to come.

"*Jeremy Brecher's* Strike! *is a classic of American historical writing. This new edition, bringing his account up to the present, comes amid rampant inequality and growing popular resistance. No book could be more timely for those seeking the roots of our current condition.*"
—Eric Foner, Pulitzer Prize winner and DeWitt Clinton Professor of History at Columbia University

"*Magnificent—a vivid, muscular labor history, just updated and rereleased by PM Press, which should be at the side of anyone who wants to understand the deep structure of force and counterforce in America.*"
—JoAnn Wypijewski, author of *Killing Trayvons: An Anthology of American Violence*

A Line in the Tar Sands: Struggles for Environmental Justice

Edited by Joshua Kahn, Stephen D'Arcy, Tony Weis, Toban Black with a Foreword by Naomi Klein and Bill McKibben

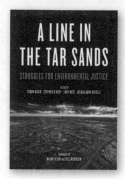

ISBN: 978-1-62963-039-7
$24.95   392 pages

Tar sands "development" comes with an enormous environmental and human cost. In the tar sands of Alberta, the oil industry is using vast quantities of water and natural gas to produce synthetic crude oil, creating drastically high levels of greenhouse gas emissions and air and water pollution. But tar sands opponents—fighting a powerful international industry—are likened to terrorists, government environmental scientists are muzzled, and public hearings are concealed and rushed.

Yet, despite the formidable political and economic power behind the tar sands, many opponents are actively building international networks of resistance, challenging pipeline plans while resisting threats to Indigenous sovereignty and democratic participation. Including leading voices involved in the struggle against the tar sands, *A Line in the Tar Sands* offers a critical analysis of the impact of the tar sands and the challenges opponents face in their efforts to organize effective resistance.

Contributors include: Greg Albo, Sâkihitowin Awâsis, Toban Black, Rae Breaux, Jeremy Brecher, Linda Capato, Jesse Cardinal, Angela V. Carter, Emily Coats, Stephen D'Arcy, Yves Engler, Cherri Foytlin, Sonia Grant, Harjap Grewal, Randolph Haluza-DeLay, Ryan Katz-Rosene, Naomi Klein, Melina Laboucan-Massimo, Winona LaDuke, Crystal Lameman, Christine Leclerc, Kerry Lemon, Matt Leonard, Martin Lukacs, Tyler McCreary, Bill McKibben, Yudith Nieto, Joshua Kahn Russell, Macdonald Stainsby, Clayton Thomas-Muller, Brian Tokar, Dave Vasey, Harsha Walia, Tony Weis, Rex Weyler, Will Wooten, Jess Worth, and Lilian Yap.

The editors' proceeds from this book will be donated to frontline grassroots environmental justice groups and campaigns.

Red Nation Rising: From Bordertown Violence to Native Liberation

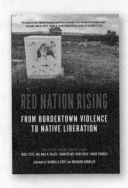

Nick Estes, Melanie K. Yazzie, Jennifer Nez Denetdale, and David Correia with a Foreword by Radmilla Cody and Brandon Benallie

ISBN: 978-1-62963-831-7 (paperback)
       978-1-629639-062 (hardcover)
$17.95/$39.95   176 pages

Red Nation Rising is the first book ever to investigate and explain the violent dynamics of bordertowns. Bordertowns are white-dominated towns and cities that operate according to the same political and spatial logics as all other American towns and cities. The difference is that these settlements get their name from their location at the borders of current-day reservation boundaries, which separate the territory of sovereign Native nations from lands claimed by the United States.

Bordertowns came into existence when the first US military forts and trading posts were strategically placed along expanding imperial frontiers to extinguish indigenous resistance and incorporate captured indigenous territories into the burgeoning nation-state. To this day, the US settler state continues to wage violence on Native life and land in these spaces out of desperation to eliminate the threat of Native presence and complete its vision of national consolidation "from sea to shining sea." This explains why some of the most important Native-led rebellions in US history originated in bordertowns and why they are zones of ongoing confrontation between Native nations and their colonial occupier, the United States.

Despite this rich and important history of political and material struggle, little has been written about bordertowns. *Red Nation Rising* marks the first effort to tell these entangled histories and inspire a new generation of Native freedom fighters to return to bordertowns as key front lines in the long struggle for Native liberation from US colonial control. This book is a manual for navigating the extreme violence that Native people experience in reservation bordertowns and a manifesto for indigenous liberation that builds on long traditions of Native resistance to bordertown violence.

The Traffic Power Structure

Planka.nu

ISBN: 978-1-62963-153-0
$12.00   96 pages

The Traffic
Power Structure
Planka.nu

The modern traffic system is ecologically unsustainable, emotionally stressful, and poses a physical threat to individuals and communities alike. Traffic is not only an ecological and social problem but also a political one. Modern traffic reproduces the rule of the state and capital and is closely linked to class society. It is a problem of power. At its core lies the notion of "automobility," a contradictory ideal of free movement closely linked to a tight web of regulations and control mechanisms. This is the main thesis of the manifesto *The Traffic Power Structure*, penned by the Sweden-based activist network Planka.nu.

Planka.nu was founded in 2001 to fight for free public transport. Thanks to creative direct action, witty public interventions, and thought-provoking statements, the network has become a leading voice in Scandinavian debates on traffic. In its manifesto, Planka.nu presents a critique of the automobile society, analyzes the connections between traffic, the environment, and class, and outlines its political vision. The topics explored along the way include Bruce Springsteen, high-speed trains, nuclear power, the security-industrial complex, happiness research, and volcano eruptions. Planka.nu rejects demands to travel ever-longer distances in order to satisfy our most basic needs while we lose all sense for proximity and community. *The Traffic Power Structure* argues for a different kind of traffic in a different kind of world.

The book has received several awards in Sweden and has been hailed by Swedish media as a "manifesto of striking analytical depth, based on profound knowledge and a will to agitation that demands our respect" (*Ny Tid*).

"The group's efficiency in evasion has created an enviable business model."
—Matt Flegenheimer, *New York Times*

"We could build a Berlin Wall around the metro stations, and they would still try to find ways to get around it."
—Jesper Pettersson, spokesperson for Stockholm's Public Transport Services

Mutual Aid: An Illuminated Factor of Evolution

Peter Kropotkin
Illustrated by N.O. Bonzo with an Introduction by David Graeber & Andrej Grubačić, Foreword by Ruth Kinna, Postscript by GATS, and an Afterword by Allan Antliff

ISBN: 978-1-62963-874-4
$20.00   336 pages

One hundred years after his death, Peter Kropotkin is still one of the most inspirational figures of the anarchist movement. It is often forgotten that Kropotkin was also a world-renowned geographer whose seminal critique of the hypothesis of competition promoted by social Darwinism helped revolutionize modern evolutionary theory. An admirer of Darwin, he used his observations of life in Siberia as the basis for his 1902 collection of essays *Mutual Aid: A Factor of Evolution*. Kropotkin demonstrated that mutually beneficial cooperation and reciprocity—in both individuals and as a species—plays a far more important role in the animal kingdom and human societies than does individualized competitive struggle. Kropotkin carefully crafted his theory making the science accessible. His account of nature rejected Rousseau's romantic depictions and ethical socialist ideas that cooperation was motivated by the notion of "universal love." His understanding of the dynamics of social evolution shows us the power of cooperation—whether it is bison defending themselves against a predator or workers unionizing against their boss. His message is clear: solidarity is strength!

Every page of this new edition of *Mutual Aid* has been beautifully illustrated by one of anarchism's most celebrated current artists, N.O. Bonzo. The reader will also enjoy original artwork by GATS and insightful commentary by David Graeber, Ruth Kinna, Andrej Grubačić, and Allan Antliff.

"N.O. Bonzo has created a rare document, updating Kropotkin's anarchist classic Mutual Aid, *by intertwining compelling imagery with an updated text. Filled with illustrious examples, their art gives the words and histories, past and present, resonance for new generations to seed flowers of cooperation to push through the concrete of resistance to show liberatory possibilities for collective futures."*
—scott crow, author of *Black Flags and Windmills* and *Setting Sights*

Between Earth and Empire: From the Necrocene to the Beloved Community

John P. Clark
with a Foreword by Peter Marshall

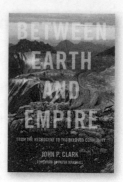

ISBN: 978-1-62963-648-1
$22.95   352 pages

Between Earth and Empire focuses on the crucial position of humanity at the present moment in Earth History. We have left the Cenozoic, the "new period of life," and are now in the midst of the Necrocene, a period of mass extinction and reversal of the course of evolution of life on Earth. We are now nearing the end of the long history of Empire and domination, faced with the alternatives of either continuing the path of social and ecological disintegration or initiating a new era of social and ecological regeneration.

The book shows that conventional approaches to global crisis on both the right and the left have succumbed to processes of denial and disavowal, either rejecting the reality of crisis entirely or substituting ineffectual but comforting gestures and images for deep, systemic social transformation. It is argued that an effective response to global crisis requires attention to all major spheres of social determination, including the social institutional structure, the social ideology, the social imaginary, and the social ethos. Large-scale social and ecological regeneration must be rooted in communities of liberation and solidarity, in which personal and group transformation take place in all these spheres, so that a culture of awakening and care can emerge.

Between Earth and Empire explores examples of significant progress in this direction, including the Zapatista movement in Chiapas, the Democratic Autonomy Movement in Rojava, indigenous movements in defense of the commons, the solidarity economy movement, and efforts to create liberated base communities and affinity groups within anarchism and other radical social movements. In the end, the book presents a vision of hope for social and ecological regeneration through the rebirth of a libertarian and communitarian social imaginary, and the flourishing of a free cooperative community globally.

"*John Clark's book is a measured manifesto. It is a must read for any activist or scholar concerned about the alternatives to capitalism's ongoing war on nature.*"
—Andrej Grubačić, coauthor of *Living at the Edges of Capitalism*